A GU

THE PROSECCO ROAD

– A SUPERIORE JOURNEY –

AMANDA MOHR

First printing: 2022

ISBN: 9798848483680

British Cataloguing Publication Data: A catalogue record of this book is available from The British Library.

Also available on Kindle.

CONTENTS

1. INTRODUCTION

On 7 July 2019, after a ten-year campaign, the hills of Prosecco di Conegliano and Valdobbiadene were inscribed as a UNESCO World Heritage Site. The inscription reads:

"Located in north-eastern Italy, the Prosecco wine production area is characterised by 'hogback' hills, ciglioni – small plots of vines on narrow grassy terraces – forests, small villages and farmland. For centuries, this rugged terrain has been shaped and adapted by man. Since the 17th century, the use of ciglioni has created a chequerboard landscape consisting of rows of vines parallel and vertical to the slopes. In the 19th century, the bellussera technique of training the vines contributed to the aesthetic characteristics of the landscape."

The Prosecco area

The UNESCO title protects the winemakers' heritage for the future, whilst also encouraging tourism.

This book journeys to Northern Italy, in particular to the very small area between the towns of Valdobbiadene and Conegliano. This, the UNESCO World Heritage Site, is the production area of the fabulous Conegliano Valdobbiadene Prosecco Superiore DOCG. The site is easily accessible from Venice airport, steeped in history and in style and tradition, and drenched in a proliferation of wonderful Prosecco wineries.

Rolling hills of the Prealps

Italy is centrally placed within Europe yet it maintains its individuality, its industriousness and its somewhat quirky sense of style. It is a deeply religious country and the epicentre of the Roman Catholic faith. Along the route we will see many examples of the legacy and maintenance of that religion: the story-telling mediaeval frescoes and the priceless works of art hidden within even the smallest village churches.

Our sparkling journey centres around the Prosecco Road. Yes, there actually is a Prosecco Road! It winds around and through the 15 municipalities that are singularly responsible for producing the finest and best Prosecco Superiore. The general Prosecco area currently produces over 500 million bottles a year. This book focuses on the best quality Prosecco: Prosecco Superiore, from the heart of the region. Prosecco Superiore accounts for just over 90 million bottles. Italy exports just under half of its Prosecco Superiore production annually; in 2021, the UK was at the top of the export list with 22% of production.

Local restaurant

This book explains a little about each municipality, the history, some interesting local events and places of interest and, most importantly, gives a list of wineries to visit. What you draw from it is up to you. Whether you use it as a guide around the area or you're a virtual traveller, an 'armchair' enthusiast, I hope it gives you some insight into this beautiful, picturesque, charming area. Be warned: the views from the hills are green, lush and absolutely breath-taking! Even the amateur photographer can't fail to get a decent panoramic vista, a fantastic photo that demonstrates the exceptional environment. No written description can do the area justice so hopefully you will find the photographs capture some of that.

Each municipality has its own identity. To see examples of enchanting mediaeval castles calls for a visit to Conegliano or

Susegana; to view the remains of early industry, head to Follina; if you would like to see traditional Italian villas there are some fabulous ones in the surrounding area. Vittorio Veneto, a lovely town to visit, retains its mediaeval charm and has countless examples of historical buildings and churches. As I mentioned, Italy is the centre of the Catholic faith and this region pays homage to that faith with many places of worship, from tiny roadside shrines to grand cathedrals. Most have history around them and beautiful Italian artistry within as well as a legendary tale or two! And there are plenty of walking trails and bicycle routes to explore in between winery visits.

Strada del Prosecco (Prosecco Road) sign

The majority of the wineries are modern in their machinery and production methods yet deeply traditional with their hospitality and their way of life. The area has exceptional local food and wine on offer: spit roasts, deli meats, cheeses, mushrooms and polenta are marvellously complemented by the outstanding DOCG Prosecco and the area's renowned local wines. Some of the wineries sell local produce, some serve it during a tasting, some have their own restaurants and a few also advertise accommodation if you want to stay in-situ.

Don't miss the coffee and cake at the many pasticcerias!

The Prosecco Superiore area sits within what is called the Marca Trevigiana area, the geographical area covered by Veneto's eastern Treviso province. Evidence has been found of some form of existence since Palaeolithic times but the earliest documentation found is Roman. The majority of recorded information comes from the arrival of the Lombards, who occupied the larger villages of the Prosecco region after the Romans. Under the guidance of Alboin, they crossed the Julian Alps in 568 AD, moving quickly along the trajectory of the Friuli and Veneto foothills, leaving garrisons in strategically significant locations with families of warriors tasked to protect the rear from possible enemy infiltration. The towns and hamlets created bore their origin from this invasion and were named accordingly. Moving from Fara Castel Roganzuolo westward, we encounter the Fara di Soligo and Fara di Valdobbiadene; on the northern side, Fara di Feltre can also be found. The word *Fara*, a derivative of the German *fahren*, indicates a nomadic unit consisting of a family group.

Local meats and cheeses

Whilst it's quite rare, there has been evidence found of Lombard burial sites. Traditionally, the dead were buried fully equipped with spears, swords and armour; however, desecration of burial land followed as sites were plundered for any valuable spoils, so the custom did not prevail.

The Lombards left an undeniable legacy. Local churches bearing the names of St Michael, St George and St Martin refer back to the Lombard period as they favoured the warrior saints' names. Also, surnames and some words of local dialect are derived from Germanic/Anglo Saxon rather than Latin beginnings. Some families encourage this continuity and proudly acknowledge Lombardian ancestry.

This region of Italy suffered desperately during the First World War and was the theatre of some intense fighting between the Italian Army and the Austro-Hungarian empire. The most horrific of these was the 1917 Battle of Caporetto, named after a town in the region, which totally ravaged the area. After more than two years of fighting, the Austro-Hungarians overwhelmed the local troops until the Italian defence line, supported by French and British troops, finally held up near the Piave River. Caporetto inflicted 300,000 casualties and produced 265,000 prisoners, temporarily improving Austria-Hungary's strategic position. Caporetto did not change the outcome of the war but its very legacy conjures up a blight in the memory of the region. WWI battle sites are acknowledged around the area.

Built and formed by this colourful history, the journey around the Prosecco DOCG area provides something for everyone: historic buildings, Italian art, quirky museums, nature trails and of course the main purpose, the fabulous Prosecco, which beckons from the proliferation of wineries scattered along the route. What is more unexpected is the multitude of photo opportunities, the steep rising hills and fabulous undulating landscapes, the lush greenness and the views around every bend in the road that literally take your breath away!

View of the Prosecco DOCG fields

Italy has more UNESCO World Heritage Sites than any other country in the world. As well as the Prosecco Superiore DOCG region, there are several other sites in the area.

Palladian Villas

Andrea Palladio, the 16th-century architect, was prolific in the region and was recognised by UNESCO in 1994. As with any trendy new design, the noble families of the area flocked to Palladio's villas, with their famous pillars and eye-catching symmetry. Subsequently, many examples of his work dot the countryside surrounding some of the smaller towns of Veneto.

Palladian villa

Pile-Dwelling Sites

Many remains of prehistoric settlements dating from between 5,000 to 500 BC have been particularly well preserved due to being submerged in wetlands. These pile-dwelling sites reveal details of trade routes, showing early transportation, including canoes and wooden wheels, some complete with axles for two-wheeled carts dating from around 3,400 BC.

Items of gold, amber and pottery, textiles and other materials – some of the earliest preserved in the world – have also been found here. This cumulative evidence has provided a unique insight into the domestic lives and settlements of some thirty different cultural groups in the Alpine area.

Livelet educational area

Longobards (Lombards) in Italy: Places of the Power (568-774 AD)

In recognition of the huge impact the Lombards had on the area and on other parts of Italy, this UNESCO award comprises seven groups of important buildings (including fortresses, churches and monasteries) found throughout the Italian Peninsula, specifically attributed to the Lombards, who migrated from northern Europe, developing their own culture and ruling over vast territories during the 6th to 8th centuries.

The Venetian Region

The Veneto region is geographically the most diverse region of Italy: it has mountains, plains, luscious tree-covered hills, Lake Garda (the largest in the country), and eventually falls away to the Adriatic Sea and the Venetian Lagoon. Throughout this area is a wide range of villages, from fortified places to alpine sites.

Revine lago

Pliny the Elder

Gaius Plinius Secundus AKA Pliny the Elder (AD 23–79) is said to be the first person to have recorded the existence of Prosecco. He was a Roman author, naturalist and philosopher and served as an army commander in the Roman Empire. He's famous for compiling the 37-volume Roman encyclopaedia *Naturalis Historia* (*Natural History*), considered the go-to authority throughout the Middle Ages. Volume 14 covered wine, including a ranking of Rome's top vineyards. Volume 17 discussed techniques in viticulture and the notion of terroir. He asserted that the vineyard exerted greater influence over wine quality than vine type, a belief still held in wine-making circles to this day.

Pliny published a rating of wines around Europe and talked about his love of wine from a place called Trieste. He called the wine 'Pucinem'. In 1593 this was referred to by Fynes Moryso, a celebrated traveller, as the first reference to Prosecco: "*Here growed the wine Pucinum, now called Prosecho, much celebrated by Pliny."* From then until recently, both the wine and the grape were called Prosecco, although to avoid confusion the grape is now officially known as the Glera grape.

Asolo at the foothills of the Italian alps

The Prosecco DOCG consortium

All the wineries listed in this book are, at the time of writing, part of the Prosecco DOCG consortium, of which membership is annual. The consortium was created back in 1962 by eleven Prosecco producers to develop and agree production regulations which would protect the quality and image of their wine.

There are three categories of members: winegrowers, wine companies and bottlers. Some producers may fit into more than one category.

A separate company, called Valoritalia, now controls all the stages of production and can sanction a producer that does not adhere to the strict regulations.

Asolo centre

The Asolo region is classed as part of the Prosecco production but is a separate denomination from the Prosecco DOCG consortium, being part of the Asolo Montello Consortium. This consortium encompasses a further 19 municipalities and other local wines, and whilst I include brief information on visiting Asolo, the book concentrates on the Conegliano Valdobbiadene Prosecco DOCG denomination.

The Prosecco DOCG consortium website has information on each winery along with a map of the area, but to get a sense of the individual wineries I would recommend you visit their individual websites. Not all Prosecco producers are open to the public, not all the tasting rooms are near the vineyards, not all producers have websites but the majority will give you facts and basic information. I would always recommend you make an appointment for a tasting visit to get the most out of the visit.

I've listed the wineries in each municipality, but some of the smaller municipalities may not have wineries within their boundaries, remaining more rural and being production area only. Some of the wineries listed have the winery and vineyard next door to each other.

All will give you a warm welcome!

2. ALL ABOUT THE PROSECCO!

You've probably chosen this book because you love Prosecco. Me too!

However, it's not until you look a little more closely that you discover there's a whole lot more to Prosecco than you first thought. There are some wonderful varieties, a range of sweetnesses and some different fizzinesses – all fabulous and all Prosecco! Hopefully this book will help you develop your thirst for more knowledge of this wonderful wine. The most difficult decision is choosing the perfect Prosecco for you.

Selection of DOCG Prosecco

Champagne has some large and recognisable brands, some more expensive than others, but we generally know what to expect when we select one of the well-known names. Prosecco hasn't really got that brand awareness. The supermarkets would have us believe that Prosecco is the brand – it's just not! There's a wide variety of different brands and sweetnesses and they're definitely not all the same; many wineries will provide you with surprisingly different taste experiences.

When I organise a tasting in the UK, I try to demonstrate and celebrate the differences, not only in the sweetness but also subtleties of taste and aroma based on the location of the vineyard and the terroir, or land, which ultimately influences the taste. Comparing two extra-dry Proseccos from different areas of the region side by side is the best way to experience this and identify which one you prefer. Ultimately, you may prefer the one you buy in the supermarket, and that's fine too. That's what's great about Prosecco. It's not about snobbery, it's about enjoying the fizziness and drinking what you love!

A tasting experience

If you're ever fortunate enough to visit the region, one thing you will discover along your journey is that Prosecco is served in Italy in a wine glass rather than a traditional flute. And of course, true to

Italian style, the wineries have their own very elegant large orb-shaped glasses. The glass is filled maybe a third full to allow the aroma to circulate and accumulate within the bowl of the glass. Taste is greatly affected by smell and drinking from a wine glass enables you to appreciate both.

Prosecco Region

All Prosecco is produced in northeastern Italy, in the Italian hills north of Venice. The total production area falls within four provinces of the Friuli Venezia Giulia region and five provinces of Veneto.

At the time of writing, the Prosecco DOCG area has over 250 wineries and more than 3,300 grape growers. This book details the members of the DOCG consortium; the majority of wineries. The focus throughout will be towards smaller, traditional, family-owned producers of the region whose vineyards lie on the bumpy, vine-filled hills, not the larger, more industrial producers from the sprawling plains.

Start of the vine's journey

Prosecco is produced using the Glera grape, described as rustic and vigorous, with hazelnut-coloured branches and rather large, loose bunches, demonstrating berries of a beautiful golden yellow. To be named Prosecco, each bottle must contain 85% of Glera grapes. It's the basis for all Prosecco and guarantees the basic structure of Conegliano-Valdobbiadene wine. Local grape varieties such as Verdiso, Perera and Bianchetta can be used to complete the structure of the wine; Pinot and Chardonnay may also be used to make up to 100%. However, the majority of Prosecco is produced using 100% Glera grapes.

Harvesting is a carefully controlled process, determined in advance by regulation and starting around mid-September in the east of the region, where the grapes have had the greatest exposure to sunlight, finishing a couple of weeks later in the west, in Valdobbiadene.

Glera grapes

Pyramid of Quality

Did you know Prosecco is graded on a pyramid of quality with six levels?

Level 1: The level 1 production area consists of 556 municipalities spread over 9 provinces. This is what I would term as 'entry level' Prosecco DOC and where the bulk of production is targeted. This is the production you're most likely to see in supermarkets.

Level 2: The next level on the pyramid of quality is based on the 95 municipalities of Treviso, which can be identified by 'Treviso' appearing somewhere on the label.

Level 3: This is followed by level 3 Prosecco: Prosecco DOC production from the wineries who produce Prosecco Superiore DOCG.

Level 4: Prosecco Superiore DOCG is different; it's not your average Prosecco. It's a world away from the everyday tipple found crammed onto the shelves in the supermarket. Every bottle at this level has 'Superiore' on the label. Level 4, DOCG Prosecco was established on April 1, 2010. The addition of the 'G' means guaranteed quality, bottle by bottle, and restrictions around the quantity of grapes imbued in this marvellous wine. (More recently, the area of Asolo has been added to the list of municipalities that produce DOCG Prosecco Superiore.)

A typical DOCG label

Level 5: Within the DOCG quality area are 43 microzones that produce Rive Prosecco, the Cru of the appellation, produced from a single vineyard in a single harvest and Level 5 on our list. Rive is an ancient term in Conegliano Valdobbiadene, denoting a steep hillside vineyard. Many Rive have been informally named for decades. Since it became an official designation in 2009, a mere 43 uniquely distinctive Rive are now designated, all with restricted production limits, which makes sampling wines from this designation a real treat. If you get offered a Rive Prosecco, do taste it! You'll find each one is unique and complex, taking their individual taste from the soil, the terroir and the microclimate of the vineyard they grow in. When I taste different Rive Prosecco, I can never pick a favourite. Each one is a delicious yet different delight depending on its origin, its sweetness, its micro-climate and its terroir.

Miotto Rive Prosecco – single vineyard, single year

San Venanzio Cartizze

Level 6: At the top of the pyramid, the pinnacle of quality, is the Cartizze Prosecco, plucked from just 106 hectares within the San Pietro di Barbozza, Santo Stefano and Saccol areas of Valdobbiadene. Cartizze Prosecco is created through the perfect combination of a mild microclimate with a particular terrain and an agricultural tradition dating back more than a thousand years. The soil on Cartizze hill is the product of different ecological eras, characterised by the presence of moraines, sandstones and clays with perfect drainage. These sublime conditions make the perfect balance for the finest of the fine! I'm told the 106 hectares is the most expensive vineyard real estate in the world. No one producer owns this area: the fortunate ones number more than a hundred growers and have several rows of vines within the Cartizze hill. Because of this, not all wineries produce Cartizze. It's a complex taste imbued with the perfect conditions of production. Around a million bottles are produced annually and, being at the top of the pyramid of quality, it's the most expensive Prosecco.

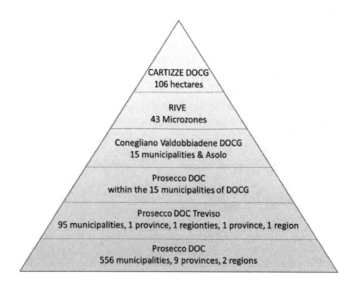

Conegliano Valdobbiadene – The Prosecco Superiore Region

The peculiarity and specialness of all DOCG Prosecco is that it's harvested by hand; those wonderful, picturesque hills don't allow for industrial machinery. It's cherished, nurtured and welcomed.

To truly appreciate the finest Prosecco, you need to head for the hills of the DOCG production area. Here you'll see the effects of the combination of south-facing slopes, the terroir, the soil composition and the sunshine, providing high daytime temperatures and contrastingly low night-time temperatures, ensuring a mixture of warm and cooler air constantly circulating, providing gentle ripening and freshness.

Prealps

The climate in the hills is not all good news, however; the young Glera grapes are delicate and visitors in May will see many vineyards with protective coverings to prevent damage that strong rains and hail can cause. A sudden hailstorm can prove devastating for the producers, ruining the harvest and perhaps preventing the production of a particular Rive in that year.

A lot of the wineries are organic; certainly they are all eco-friendly, and biologico Prosecco is marketed, where specialism is given to produce a completely natural product. Traditional methods to monitor the health of the vines are also used. For example, some wineries plant roses at the end of the rows of vines; if the rose is healthy, it follows the vines must also be healthy.

Bortolin Angelo rose

Prosecco as an Appellation

Prosecco has an intense, aromatic and fragrant flavour, and can have hints of yellow or green apple, pear, white peach, apricot, wisteria and acacia, the nose being influenced by the terroir and conditions. It has intense primary aromas most often described as fresh and light.

We're all familiar with the fabulous pop of the cork and the delightful, creamy effervescence a bottle of Prosecco is famous for. However, Prosecco is an appellation, not a single wine, so it comes in a variety of different species.

Spumante

Firstly, and most popular, is Prosecco spumante, vigorously sparkling and anywhere between 4.5 – 5.5 bars of pressure, which is responsible for producing all that foamy fizziness.

Frizzante

You may have come across Prosecco with a screw cap, or with a bare cork held together with a piece of string. This is Prosecco frizzante, a legacy wine, less foamy than the Spumante but still sparkling; it's likely to be around a maximum of 2.5 bars of pressure. Traditionally, workers used to drink frizzante Prosecco diluted with lemon water to quench their thirst whilst working in the fields at harvest time.Tranquillo

Tranquillo

A less well-known variety is 'still' Prosecco (Tranquillo). Less than 3% of Prosecco produced are Tranquillo. It's not completely still, exuding 1 bar of pressure, which gives it a slight movement. It's produced in a bottle more known for white wine and usually requires a corkscrew to open. It's a classy elegant wine, and because it has fewer bubbles it is much softer on the palate and stomach.

Sui Lieviti/Col Fondo

This is the name of the traditional Prosecco, once again becoming more popular as wineries widen their product offerings. Production volumes are small as it's produced by the more expensive classic method, where the second fermentation takes place in the bottle, with the yeasts forming a natural sediment and making the wine a little cloudy in appearance. It's a niche product made by an artisanal technique and is generally made in Brut Nature style.

Compared to a classic Prosecco it is less fruity, less of an apple-type aroma and a much yeastier smell and flavour. Recently added to the production regulations, it is also termed Col Fondo, roughly translated as 'with sediment'. It has very fine bubbles and is quite full, fresh and gutsy on the palate. Though lacking in the elegance of some of the other versions, it displays some of the same basic characteristics, along with a notably appealing flavour.

Just to add more confusion, Prosecco also comes in a variety of sweetnesses. Varieties currently produced are:

Extra Brut (or Brut zero), which has anything between zero and 6g/ltr residual sugar

Brut, which can have up to 12g of residual sugar

Extra Dry, between 12-17g of residual sugar

Dry, between 17-32g of residual sugar.

It surprises most people to find out that Extra Dry is sweeter than

Brut. The majority of people will be used to drinking the Extra Dry Prosecco, as it is the biggest production and the one usually found in supermarkets – but it is sweeter than the Brut version!

Don't be drawn by the marketing of 'skinny' Prosecco – all Extra Brut and Brut Prosecco have fewer calories than a glass of wine and about the same calories as so called 'skinny' Prosecco.

Prosecco hills

3. THE WINERIES – PLAN YOUR TRIP

Your visit to the region is likely to be quite short, maybe a couple of days or even a day trip, so it's important to get the most out of your visit.

There are almost too many wineries to choose from. Not all wineries accept visitors or do tastings – but there's plenty of choice as the area has so many. It would be impossible to mention every single one, and probably more than a little confusing if I attempted to describe them all in detail. You will enjoy an enthusiastic welcome from every winery you come across but to get the most out of your visit it would be better to do some initial research and book an appointment with the winery. Hopefully the following chapters will give you some insight and a little information to help you do so.

Visits can take up to two hours, depending on whether you opt for a tour of the production process or not, so make sure to allow for this when booking and specify what you want to see/taste if possible. Some of the wineries offer a vineyard walk. Remember: this is a hilly area where grapes are handpicked due to the nature of the terrain.

Restaurant in Conegliano

Your travel arrangements and the length of your trip will most likely determine where you stay. The region has many fine places, from 4-star accommodation to something a little more rustic in the form of an agriturismo. If you have your own transport, you can pretty much choose anywhere in the region. If you're travelling without a vehicle, I would probably recommend a stay in Conegliano. It's a short train journey from Venice and has many central hotels with several others on the outskirts. Conegliano also has plenty of good restaurants. There's a taxi rank outside the railway station or your hotel can organise one. The chapter on Conegliano has wineries listed in the town. Ask your hotel for transport options if you want to travel further afield.

Agriturismo

The DOCG Consortium website lists its member wineries in size categories:

- Production of up to 150,000 bottles
- Production of between 100,000 and 500,000 bottles
- Production of between 500,000 and 1,000,000 bottles

- Production of over 1,000,000 bottles.

www.prosecco.it/en/wineries

The website also details opening times of the wineries and informs on what type of offering each winery has. The list isn't always entirely up to date as it's dependent on the information submitted by the individual wineries, but it encompasses:

Wine Tasting	E-commerce	Accommodation
Restaurant	Retail Sales	Sale of Local
Winery Visits	Vineyard Visits	Food Products

It's time to make a decision on what you're looking for on your Prosecco visit. Do you want to tromp around vineyards, are you interested in learning the production methods or do you just want to drink and enjoy quality Prosecco? Perhaps you would like to learn more about Prosecco and pairings with local food? There's something for everyone – but you should try and choose a winery that offers your particular requirements.

If you opt for one that advertises wine tastings, that's what you will get – but don't be disappointed if you find yourself in a shop or a retail space selling different products. Not all wine tastings are conducted in wineries, just as not all wineries are open to the public. The winemakers love you to appreciate their products and will give you endless information but the tasting service is chargeable and the price is dependent on the individual wineries. And if you don't book in advance, you may turn up during a busy period and might not be able to have a tasting. Also remember that August is a holiday period in Italy, when some wineries close, and September is harvest time, the busiest period for the winemakers. Wineries set their own opening times and not all are open on Sundays.

Vineyard on a hillside

I particularly enjoy the wineries that accompany the Prosecco with small tastes of local produce, in particular bread, cheese and local hams. It seems to work so well and you might leave a winery feeling like you've eaten and drunk sufficient to last you the rest of the day.

The hosts are winemakers through and through, as their parents before them. They are likely to have been to the Oenological School to study or could be qualified sommeliers. They know their stuff, take real pride in it, and their knowledge will encompass not only Prosecco but also many varieties of local wine. On your visit you will definitely taste fabulous Prosecco, but you may also enjoy tasting some of the local wines. Doing this, I've discovered a real liking for Verdiso, one of the region's white wines, which is sometimes used within Prosecco production but is also bottled separately and is delicious in its own right. There are also several local red wines produced; Marzemino is one. A famous Italian drink, grappa, can be found locally along with a speciality of Refrontolo: passito, a sweet wine, produced from dried grape skins. Don't be afraid to try the red passito, a Christmas cake-tasting syrupy wine, delicious with local cheese.

Local products to try with Prosecco

The majority of wineries in the region are family businesses, or have a legacy associated with family. Some of the large wineries ask for a minimum number of people for a tour. You could be escorted around a substantial production process by a member of staff rather than a direct owner. I tend to steer away from the very large wineries, preferring smaller ones maintained and run by family members, who really project the passion they feel about their vines and land. They do employ staff, of course, but their presentations are less process driven and more individual.

Smaller wineries may also give you a tour of the production process, which could be half a dozen huge tanks, and you might also see the giant hopper to which the grapes are delivered. It's a great opportunity to understand the process but bear in mind how many times you want to see this end-to-end experience. When I tour, I select one winery for the production process, a different winery for a vineyard walk, and other wineries for a simple tasting and possibly lunch.

Charmat method of Prosecco production

Some of the smaller producers work as an agriturismo. This is a working farm that produces, among other things, a little bit of Prosecco alongside homegrown food stuffs and offers accommodation in a rustic, rural environment. Each one is different, but it's an opportunity to see the workings of a farm and embrace the rural lifestyle. Most of the agriturismo are small with a few rooms, possibly with shared facilities; some of the more established ones may have their own pool, but mostly it will be akin to staying on a farm.

Other wineries offer Relais accommodation on-site (equivalent to a 4 star). This is much more upmarket than the rustic agriturismo with a finer, more elegant offering, almost like a villa stay. In most instances it's unlikely to be co-located with the winery but may be somewhere nearby.

It's easy to say, but don't try to do too many Prosecco tastings. Take time to select something that appeals to you. If you've got your own transport, I would suggest picking a winery from the east – say, Refrontolo or Conegliano – and one or two from Valdobbiadene (which has the most wineries of the region) in the west. Combine your visit with some other local attractions or take lunch in the area as you travel.

4. THE TECHNICAL BIT

All Prosecco is made under strict Prosecco DOC regulations and guidelines.

In order to maintain high standards of quality and protect the image of Prosecco, the consortium introduced a number of measures under DOC regulations in 2009. New laws restricted the area of production and gave the principal grape a new name, Glera. Importantly, the new regulations mean that Prosecco has been transformed into a geographical location, exclusively, just like Champagne, so the name cannot be used for wines made outside this area or without following these DOC regulations:

- Region of production: north-east Italy – Veneto and Friuli
- Grape variety: Glera (previously known as Prosecco) must make up 85% of bottle contents
- Method of sparkling wine production: Charmat (tank fermentation)
- DOC Prosecco can be still, frizzante or spumante
- Two sub zones: Treviso (in the Veneto) and Trieste (in Friuli)
- Two DOCG regions: Conegliano Valdobbiadene and Asolo or Colli Asolani
- Four sweetness levels
    - Extra Brut – less than 6g/l sugar
    - Brut – less than 12g/l sugar
    - Extra Dry – between 12 and 17g/l sugar
    - Dry – between 17 and 32g/l sugar
- In 2009, the IGT wine region on the flat lands was upgraded to DOC status
- Wines produced outside the DOC and DOCG zones may no longer be called Prosecco and can be called 'Glera' instead

Previously all Prosecco produced had to be white to meet the criteria established by the consortium. However, in May 2020, the rules were amended to incorporate a brand-new type of Prosecco, a rosé Prosecco. This change was approved by the Ministry of Agricultural, Food and Forestry Policies' National Wine Committee. (This change only allows for DOC production and the DOCG level Prosecco is still only allowed as a white Prosecco.)

First production of Prosecco DOC Rosé appeared on retail shelves in late 2020. The consortium estimates the total production of rosé could amount to more than 30 million bottles per year, with 16.8 million bottles produced from the first harvest.

Bottling

Production Process

It is of vital importance for any production method that the starting grapes are of excellent quality and perfectly healthy. The grapes must come from well-located, well exposed soils and from vineyards with the requisite buds per plant. Harvesting the grapes must take place before they are yet perfectly ripe in order to obtain a base wine with a lower alcohol content and more sustained acidity. The high acidity of 'sparkling wine' is required to obtain a product that then lasts over time.

Prosecco DOCG can be produced by the traditional (classic) method or by the Charmat-Martinotti method.

The Charmat-Martinotti method, the most popular method of Prosecco production, was invented by Federico Martinotti at the end of the 1800s, and is the method used to obtain less expensive sparkling and semi-sparkling wines. It allows for the production of sparkling wines whilst retaining the flavour of the base wine. In 1910, the Frenchman Eugène Charmat built and patented the first pressure-tight tank, an autoclave. After the first fermentation, the resulting base wine is transferred into sealed tanks where, with the addition of yeasts, the residual sugar generates pressure as the carbon dioxide dissolves in the wine. To achieve the perfect balance between taste, aroma, consistency and size of bubbles, the wine is kept in these tanks for at least 20 days and can be for as long as 6 months. The temperature in the tanks can be decreased to stop fermentation or increased to re-start the process. The Charmat-Martinotti method has proved to be much faster and is more widely used for economic reasons. Italians suggest light-heartedly that whilst they did the hard work the French did the paperwork, as the Italian Martinotti's original idea was patented by the Frenchman, Charmat. Hence the classification of the name as either Charmat or Charmat-Martinotti.

The classic method, as its name suggests, has its roots in the ancient history of wine making, where the second fermentation takes place in the bottle. Used more for Su Lieveti production, after the first fermentation a mixture of wine, yeast and sugar is added to the base wine, which is decanted into bottles. The bottles are closed and stacked horizontally in a cool constant temperature. After around forty days, the yeast autolysis starts and lasts for a minimum of nine months. The bottles are matured in A-framed racks called *pupitres*. They are turned every day until ready to be inverted in a vertical position to collect the yeast sediment in the crown cap. Once this riddling process is completed, with the disgorgement, the neck of the bottle is frozen to -20°C, the crown cap is removed and the sediment ejects, thanks to the pressure naturally created inside the bottle. The bottles can then be sealed, usually with a cork, in order to be released for retailing. This method is used to produce Su Lieveti or Col Fondo (traditional Prosecco with some of the yeast remaining in the bottle).

Prosecco tanks

Conegliano is the home of Italy's oldest wine school, founded in 1876. The winemakers take their work very seriously, and the majority have been trained or have some connection with the school. The school works in conjunction with wineries, supplying students for research activities and combining knowledge to improve production and housekeeping efforts. The overriding premise of production is to grow vines as organically as possible. Alongside the oenologists are the sommeliers, the marketeers and the business people. Most families have to be a little of all of the above.

I am often asked what the difference is between Prosecco, Cava and Champagne. Apart from the obvious geographical one, the method used in producing Prosecco is totally different from Champagne and Cava, as their production utilises the traditional or classic method. Here's a potted view:

Length of aging

Champagne is aged much longer and because of the method, the quality matures with time. Prosecco has a two-fermentation process but does not improve with age. It should be enjoyed when it is young and fresh.

Taste palate

Because Champagne has much more contact with the yeast (separate bottles and time) than Prosecco does in a tank, the primary tastes of Champagne are citrus, peach, white cherry, almond, and toast. Prosecco embodies the flavours of honeydew melon, pear, green apple, honeysuckle, and cream.

Bubbles

Prosecco is produced under much less pressure, which causes the bubbles to be much lighter, frothier, and less persistent. Champagne, on the other hand, is produced in individual bottles, under immense pressure — the bubbles that are produced are fine, very persistent and sharp.

Economics

Due to the time-consuming, detailed process by which Champagne is produced, the price is generally higher than Prosecco. The large tanks used in Prosecco production allow winemakers to produce more quickly and on a larger scale.

Other Local Grapes

The yield for production of DOC is grapes harvested to a yield no greater than 12 tonnes per hectare. The finished wine must attain a minimum alcohol level of 12% for red wines and 10.5% for whites in order to be labelled with the Colli di Conegliano DOC designation.

Prosecco grapes

The red wine is a blend made up of Merlot, Cabernet Sauvignon, Cabernet Franc, Marzemino and Incrocio Manzoni 2.15 (a recently crossbred grape variety). The wine has to be aged at least two years prior to being released.

Refrontolo passito is made up of at least 95% Marzemino with up to 5% of other local non-aromatic varieties allowed. The dry white of the DOC passito is made from at least 30% Manzoni Bianco with between 30-70% of Pinot Blanc and Chardonnay and up to 10% total of Sauvignon Blanc and/or Riesling Renano.

5. CONEGLIANO

Number of inhabitants: 35,231
Altitude: 74m
Area km²: 36.38
Patron Saint: Leonard of Noblac – Nov 6

Conegliano is a town and municipality about 30km north of Treviso. With excellent rail connections to both Venice and Treviso, it is situated in a prime location close to the Prealps. The city has the largest population of the Prosecco DOCG area.

In the last decade, the city and its territory has focused on developing its wine making. Conegliano devotes about 30% of the municipal area to vineyards, with an average size of plot of one hectare. The growing development of this sector is due in particular to the presence of the Wine School, founded in 1876 by GB Cerletti and A Carpenè. Within the campus are the Professional Institute of Agriculture, the Agricultural Technical Institute, the Regional Centre for Viticulture, Wine and Grappa of Veneto Agriculture and the DOC Consortium of the Province.

Conegliano has good transport links: two motorways run quite close to the town (the A27 and A28), and two airports (Treviso and Venice) are around an hour away, by car or train. If you're staying in Venice and want to visit the Prosecco area, it is possible to get a train direct from Venice to Conegliano. The train takes an hour and a return costs around €10, with a regular service throughout the day. A lot of the wineries in Conegliano are 10-20 minutes away from the town centre; there's a taxi stand outside Conegliano station. It's so close it's really achievable. It's a world away from the hustle and bustle of Venice, a complete contrast. In the Wineries section I've recommended a couple of options for those visiting for a day on public transport.

If you're staying overnight, there are a few central hotels to choose from and many more in the surrounding area. This allows it to accommodate a steady stream of tourists keen to tour the wine routes.

Conegliano

From Conegliano the first Italian wine tour, the 'Wine Route Prosecco' – now called the Prosecco Road – and Colli Conegliano Valdobbiadene (1966), and the latest 'Wine Route Piave' were born.

Conegliano

History

Conegliano has been occupied in some form for over 1,000 years. Evidence of early activity can be seen in the Castle Museum. But it was not until the invasion of the Lombards that structure was founded and an element of protection given to the inhabitants. The gravitational element of the castle made it the centre of activity and an early municipal government was formed which was strengthened and renewed, along with new fortifications, when the town was governed by the Ezzelini and Scaligeri families.

The town became part of the Republic of Venice in 1337. Fortification of the castle continued through the centuries and changes in occupation. The castle was finally demolished in the 18th century, leaving just the castle keep intact and providing stone for newer buildings.

Conegliano castle

The construction of the railway inevitably moved the nucleus of the town further south. Conegliano and the Veneto region were once part of Austria, eventually becoming part of the unified Italy in 1866.

Conegliano castle

Feasts

Every June, a spectacular chess or 'dama' game, known as the *Dama Castellana*, is performed in the historical centre of Conegliano where the pieces are represented by actual people. It's not an historical event, having been introduced quite recently, but it has been adopted as a traditional event in the Coneglianese calendar.

Locals are invited to audition for the opportunity to dress in mediaeval clothes and participate in this colourful event, representing pieces of the chess board.

The event features jousting and tournaments reliving the charm of ancient duels between knights, ready to challenge for a betrothal or to acquire valuable land.

Dama Castellana

There is also a Conegliano Summer Festival, with theatre, music and readings, and the Fall Coneglianese, with the festival associations.

The Grape Festival symbolises the close ties Conegliano has with its wine-growing region and takes place in the centre of Conegliano. It's a whole month of festivities throughout August, commencing with a music festival 'on the streets of Prosecco' by Yuri Bashmet, its artistic director, the greatest violist in the world today, and incorporating Prosecco: the local success story.

Places of Interest

Conegliano's historical legacy can be seen in everyday life in the city. The beautifully preserved Contrada Grande – the original main street, Via XX Settembre – was the heart of the mediaeval city, surrounded by city walls and accessed via one of the three gates: Porta del Rujo in the west, Porta del Monticano in the east and the southerly Porta San Polo.

The Porta del Monticano was first referred to in documents as early as 1309. It still retains its original marking showing a fresco depicting the 'Lion of St. Mark andante' by Giovanni Antonio de Sacchis, AKA Pordenone (1483-1539). Now slightly faded in glory and restored over the years by Scaligeri and Carraresi, it's still eternally displayed on the thoroughfare.

The symbolism behind the lion is supposed to show the Venetian Republic ready to conquer the mainland. It is said that the open book the lion holds between its legs is a symbol of the peaceful process with which the city was subjected to the Serenissima (Venetian Republic).

Porta del Monticano

Any visit to Conegliano must take in the Via XX Settembre. It's a quietly elegant street, replete with fascinating buildings, colourful frescoes and covered tiled walkways, or loggia, protecting the visitor from the elements but giving the Italian city some undisputed chic. It's beautiful, a classy example of an ancient mediaeval city, and reminds me a little of more popular tourist spots like Dubrovnik.

Via XX Settembre

The Renaissance palaces include the ancient Monte di Pietà, characterised by a fresco that covers the entire façade with angels among clouds, supporting the instruments of the Passion. A little further on, on the opposite side of the road, stands Palazzo Montalban Nuovo, an imposing building of the 18th century.

Make sure to stop in one of the plethora of cafés or eateries to enjoy the atmosphere. There's an excellent cafe by the porticoed passage between the Contrada and Piazza delle Pecorelle (now Piazza IV Novembre).

Along the Via XX Settembre, there are two other noteworthy buildings: Palazzo Sarcinelli and Casa Longega. The first was the home of the noble Sarcinelli family of Ceneda from the first half of the 16th century. It has an airy loggia on the ground floor and a hall on the main floor decorated with stuccoes that display portraits of the most important visitors. The 15th century Casa Longega was the first residence of the ancient and noble Montalban family, as shown by the coat of arms on the column capitals. Next to the building is Via Marcatelli, which leads to Porta San Polo, also called 'del pidocchio', taking the visitor outside the city walls.

The wealth of Renaissance buildings and their history can be confusing as they sit side by side on the same street. Luckily, the tourist information centre is also found here so more detailed information is available if you want to delve further into the history of these magnificent buildings.

Piazza Cima

Halfway along the street is the Piazza Cima, which overlooks the Palazzo del Municipio, designed in the 18th century by Ottavio

Scotti. Also around the square is the Academy Theatre, a work of the mid-19th century, and the 16th century Palazzo da Collo. On the left of the Academy, you can see the beautiful pierced balcony of Casa Sbarra, whose façade still shows traces of the frescoes that once completely covered it.

Opposite Piazza Cima is the largest Piazzetta, built in 1866, which overlooks Casa Dalla Balla, again highly decorated with remarkable frescoes, stone cornices and a corner balcony.

Piazzetta

The Duomo di Conegliano (Cathedral), a fantastically statuesque building, can be found nestled among the other opulent buildings along this road. Its construction was started in 1345 by the Battuti, a religious order originating from Umbria, in the centre of a hospice for pilgrims.

The outside of the cathedral is notable for the frescoes, painted by Ludovico Toeput in the late 16th century.

Inside the church there are notable works of art: the altarpiece was painted by Cima da Conegliano, the celebrated local painter, and other pieces include works by Palma il Giovane and Francesco Frigimelica. The Sala dei Battuti is a beautiful rectangular room off to the right-hand side of the cathedral with a whole range of frescoes, mostly painted by Francesco da Milano around 1530.

Conegliano Cathedral (Duomo)

The Castle of Conegliano remains a symbol of Conegliano and its tower (Torre della Guardia), the only part of the castle that remains, dominates the city and its surroundings. The easy route to visit is by car; it is within walking distance of the city but involves a hill climb for those who choose to try to it. The 11th century castle area incorporates mediaeval gateways and newly restored walls and leads the visitor to the expansive garden area. From here, there are magnificent views over the city and across the beautiful countryside that surrounds it.

Walls of Conegliano

The tower is now home to the Civic Museum, which is cheap to enter and displays an excellent collection of armour, curios and archaeological finds. It houses many works of art. A fresco by Giovanni Antonio Pordenone dated around 1514, originally found in the San Antonio Abate church, stands out. It depicts the Magdalene, St. Catherine and two other saints. There is also a series of three frescoes, works of the 15th century, respectively depicting the Madonna Enthroned with Saints, the Crucifixion and the Last Supper. Access to the top of the keep is through the museum with yet more excellent 360-degree views.

Conegliano castle museum

Relax in the gardens and enjoy a coffee or Prosecco from the adjoining café. There's also a restaurant on site.

Castle café

WINERIES

BIANCAVIGNA S. S. SOC. AGRICOLA

via Montenero, 8/c Conegliano
+390438788403 | +390438789721
info@biancavigna.it | www.biancavigna.it

Wine tastings, retail sales, sale of local food products, winery & vineyard visits
Production is listed as between 100,000 and 500,000 bottles

BORGO ANTICO

via Strada delle Spezie, 39 Conegliano
+390438788111
info@borgoanticovini.com | www.borgoanticovini.com

Wine tastings, retail sales, winery and vineyard visits
Production up to 150,000 bottles

Borgo Antico vines

I arranged to visit this winery during the busiest time of the year for them, directly after the harvest. My host (and owner) Leonardo was informative and gracious. Starting on a sunny terrace overlooking the vineyard, he described the fields of vines and soil composition. This was followed by a superb tasting of fine quality Prosecco in the small tasting room. I imagine larger parties would probably use the outside terrace, but at 9am on a cool Saturday morning I didn't long for the outside space!

Borgo Antico tasting

Leonardo took me through his range of Prosecco, opening fresh bottles for each one. The Extra Brut, Rive di Ogliano was particularly special. I immediately bought a bottle and would recommend incorporating this winery on your trip.

Be aware, the satnav takes you past the winery, which hasn't got any visible branding, but is on the road side so clearly visible. It's just over 4 miles from Conegliano so within easy reach by taxi.

Tasting room at Borgo Antico

CA' VITTORIA
Strada delle Caneve, 34, Conegliano, TV, Italia
+39043863851
info@cavittoria.com | www.cavittoria.com

Wine tastings, retail sales, winery & vineyard visits
Production up to 150,000 bottles

I visited this winery, without an appointment and speaking only English. It was one of my earlier trips on a food pairing mission, looking for a Prosecco to pair with pork. The owner was quickly summoned from out in the fields. As I explained my problem, he brought out several Proseccos and a sparkling rosé. He then proceeded to search his own fridge and produced some spicy pork and a hunk of fresh bread so I could create the experience of a food pairing. I loved the rosé – it suited the pork really well – but back then it couldn't be classed as a Prosecco.

I decided to buy a bottle, at which point he waved away my attempts to purchase, giving me the bottle I was so impressed with. As I said goodbye, profusely thanking him, he jumped back on his tractor and resumed his day's work! This generosity of spirit amazes me but is somewhat typical of the area.

Again, this winery is quite close to the city, just under 4 miles.

Generous hospitality at Ca' Vittoria

CANTINA DI CONEGLIANO E VITTORIO VENETO
Via del Campardo, 3, Vittorio Veneto, TV, Italia
Vittorio Veneto +390438500209
Conegliano +39043822268
info@cantinavittorio.it, info@cantinadiconegliano.it |
www.cantinavittorio.it

Wine tastings, retail sales, winery visits
Production listed as up to 150,000 bottles

CARMINA LOGGIA DEL COLLE srl
Via Mangesa, 10, Conegliano, TV, Italia
+39043823719 | +390438411974
info@carmina.it | www.carmina.it

Wine tastings, retail sales, winery visits
Production listed as between 100,000 and 500,000 bottles

Drive to Carmina winery

What a beautiful drive to the winery – and it's so close to Conegliano! Just 2 miles from the railway station.

I was met by Massimo, who gave me the history of the winery. Apparently, his grandfather was posted to the area during the war and loved it so much he returned to settle here.

Looking at the photo above, taken on the drive to the winery, it's easy to see why.

Looking from the winery

Carmina winery

CARPENÈ MALVOLTI spa
Via Antonio Carpenè, Conegliano, TV, Italia
+39 0438 364611 | +39 0438 364690
info@carpene-malvolti.com | www.carpene-malvolti.com

Wine tastings, retail sales, winery visits
Production listed as over 1,000,000 bottles

Carpenè Malvolti, the historical firm of Italian Oenology, was founded in 1868 by Antonio Carpenè who decided to make sparkling wines with the grapes harvested from the hills of the Conegliano and Valdobbiadene area. It was a dream that has become a mission, now in its 5th generation. This was the first winery in Italy to produce Prosecco as a sparkling wine.

CASA TERRIERA
Via Immacolata di Lourdes 92/a Conegliano
+393922613887
info@casaterriera.it | www.casaterriera.it

Retail sales, winery visits
Production listed as up to 150,000 bottles

SOC. AGR. GLI ALLORI
Via delle Caneve, Collalbrigo, Conegliano
+393463075380
info@gliallori.eu | www.gliallori.eu

Wine tasting, retail sales, sale of local food products, vineyard visits
Production up to 150,000 bottles

L'ANTICA QUERCIA

Via Cal di Sopra 8, Scomigo di Conegliano
+390438789344
info@anticaquercia.it | www.anticaquercia.it

Wine tastings, retail sales, sale of local food products, winery &
vineyard visits
Production listed as up to 150,000 bottles

The winery

I'm always pleasantly surprised to find a hidden gem. I spent a
lovely afternoon here on a wine tasting mission. Giulia took us on a
vineyard walk up to the two oak trees that form the name of the
winery. The views – gently sweeping rows of vines with the far-
reaching Prealps dominating in the distance – are stunning and
idyllic. We did our tasting after a short walk into the vineyard, sat
among the vines under a parasol next to a converted wine barrel
that housed a couple of bench seats and a wine cooler (obviously for
less than perfect days). We tried the Colfondo and the Brut. The
winery is fully organic; Giulia explained the processes used. A

testament to the quality is that I immediately bulk ordered and can see this winery becoming a firm favourite for future visits. L'Antica Quercia is just over 5 miles from Conegliano.

Tasting table for two at Antica Quercia

Outside Antica Quercia

VINICOLTURA LE RUGHE
Via Papa Giovanni XXIII, 24, Conegliano, TV, Italia
+39043475033 | +390434754606
www.proseccolerughe.eu

Wine tastings, retail sales, winery & vineyard visits
Production listed as between 100,000 and 500,000 bottles

LUCCHETTA MARCELLO Soc. Agr.
Via Calpena, 38, Conegliano, TV, Italia
+39043832564 | +39043835279
info@lucchettavini.com | www.lucchettavini.com

Wine tastings, retail sales
Production up to 150,000 bottles

MASOTTINA
Via Custoza, 2, Conegliano, TV, Italia
+390438400775 | +390438402034
info@masottina.it | www.masottina.it

Wine tastings, retail sales
Production between 100,000 and 500,000 bottles

I purchased their organic Prosecco through a website that delivered to the UK. It's quite a fruity offering and was lively and pleasant.

SAN GIOVANNI Az. Vin. di Perini Giovanni e C.
Via Manzana, 4, Moro, Conegliano, TV, Italia
+39043831598 | +39043835300
vinisangiovanni@libero.it | www.vinicolasangiovanni.it

Wine tastings, retail sales and winery visits
Production between 100,000 and 500,000 bottles

GB CERLETTI AGRICULTURAL TECHNICAL INSTITUTE

via XXVIII Aprile, 20 Conegliano

+39043861524 | +390438450403

scuolaenologica@isisscerletti.it | www.scuolaenologica.it

Established in 1876, the wine school is part of one of the most important training centres in Italy. Equipped with modern facilities, it produces many wines, including those obtained from the crossbreeds created by Prof. Manzoni. It produces a total of 50,000 bottles annually, including 11,000 of Conegliano Valdobbiadene Prosecco Superiore. Sale and visits throughout the year.

TENUTA DEGLI ULTIMI

Via Generale Armando Diaz, 18, Conegliano, TV, Italia

+39043832888

ultimo@degliultimi.it | www.degliultimi.it

Open to the public but no further information given.

VIGNE DORO società

Via Guizza, 44, Conegliano, TV, Italia

+390438410108

info@vignedoro.it | www.vignedoro.it

Wine tastings, winery visits
Production listed as up to 150,000 bottles

VINICOLA SERENA srl

Via Camillo Bianchi, 1, 31015 Scomigo TV, Italia

+3904382011 | +390438394935

info@vinicolaserena.com | www.vinicolaserena.com

Open to the public
Production over 1,000,000 bottles

ZARDETTO
Via Martiri delle Foibe, 18, Scomigo, Conegliano, TV, Italia
+390438394969
info@zardettoprosecco.com | zardettoprosecco.com

Wine tastings, retail sales, winery & vineyard visits
Production over 1,000,000 bottles

6. SAN VENDEMIANO

Number of inhabitants: 9,961
Altitude: 51m
Area km²: 18.51
Patron Saint: San Vendemiale – Jun 1

Dwarfed by Conegliano less than 5 miles away, San Vendemiano's historic legacy was built on the Catholic religion and some fine works of art synonymous with Italian churches, which can be seen in the Chiesa di San Pietro in Vincoli (Church of St Peter in Chains) in Zoppe and the Parish Church in Vendemiano. It is a small municipality approximately 3.6 km from Conegliano and the second stop on our wine route. For the last 800 years, its fortunes have been closely tied to that of Conegliano.

View from Conegliano castle

History

San Vendemiano is named after the African bishop San Vendemiale who was martyred by the Vandals (a barbaric tribe that expanded across Europe in 400 AD) and whose worship has been associated with San Fiorenzo since ancient times. In the 7th century, relics of the two saints were brought from Corsica to Treviso, where it is said they are still kept by the Bishop of Treviso.

Notable Locals

Alessandro Del Piero, a former professional footballer and now a respected pundit, was born in San Vendemiano in 1974. Del Piero is widely regarded by players and managers as one of the greatest Italian players of all time, winning the Italian award for footballer of the year in 1998 and 2008. Del Piero has scored in every competition in which he has participated. He was included in a 2004 poll, a list of the 125 greatest living footballers selected by Pele as a part of FIFA's centenary celebrations. In the same year, he was also voted into the UEFA Golden Jubilee Poll, a list of the 50 best European players of the past 50 years.

WINERIES

Two wineries can be found in San Vendemiano.

FURLAN
Vicolo Saccon, 48, Saccon, San Vendemiano, TV, Italia
+390438778267 | +390438478996
info@furlanvini.com | www.furlanvini.com

Wine tasting, accommodation, retail sales, winery & vineyard visits
Production up to 150,000 bottles

Furlan entry sign

They have a full product range of local wines: whites and reds and two Prosecco DOCG; one is an Extra Dry Prosecco and the other is a frizzante. They also have a variety of DOC Prosecco and sparkling rosé to sample. We called by appointment and met Monia, a sommelier and expert wine buff, who talked us through her selection of Prosecco and wines. The visit was definitely enjoyable and informative and gave us an opportunity to taste native wines as well as Prosecco.

The winery is 3 miles from Conegliano, so quite accessible by taxi.

MACCARI SPUMANTE
Via Olivera, 21, Conegliano
Contact: +39 0438 400350
spumanti@maccarivini.it

Retail sales, winery visits
Production is listed as between 100,000 and 500,000 bottles.

7. COLLE UMBERTO

Number of inhabitants: 5,071
Altitude: 144m
Area km²: 13.58
Patron Saint: Saint Thomas – July 3

Colle Umberto is located about 60 km north of Venice and about 30 km north of Treviso. Called 'Colle' until 1867 because of its position on a hill, its name was changed following a visit by King Vittorio Emanuele II and Crown Prince Umberto.

Colle and the hamlet of San Martino are situated on two hills of morainic origin at 145 metres above sea level, about 10 km from the Venetian Prealps. At the top of the hill stands the town hall and below it the parish church of San Tomaso Apostolo, built between 1806 and 1809, and the bell tower of 1816. The hamlet is crossed by the Meschio River, which has played an important role in its economy; some of the mills built along its course are still in use.

Colle Umberto

History

Colle Umberto has been inhabited since prehistoric times, as attested by numerous archaeological finds dating back to the Paleovenetian civilization. Its early importance was signified by the founding of an abbey, now re-purposed as the town hall, dedicated to San Pietro Apostolo (St Peter the Apostle), by the Crociferi Fathers. The abbey is mentioned in documents over a dispute between religious groups in 1154.

Colle and San Martino were part of the Caminesi fiefdom until 1337 when they too passed to the Venetian Republic, remaining there until 1797. During this period, thanks to the safety and well-being guaranteed by the Serenissima, Colle became a place of great interest, probably the reason why it was chosen by many families of the Venetian nobility to erect their country houses in the municipality.

Villa Verecondi – Scortecci

Places of Interest

Colle Umberto is famous for its villas, which can be viewed around the area – although most of these are in private hands so tours are not possible.

Whilst the area has a great deal of vines, no wineries are established in this municipality.

Villa - Castello Lucheschi

8. VITTORIO VENETO

Number of inhabitants: 28,148
Altitude: 145m
Area km²: 82.80
Patron Saint: San Titian and Santa Augusta of Treviso – Jan 16, Aug 22

Within Treviso, Vittorio Veneto is the largest city by area. Located on the southern side of the Belluno Prealps, around 145 metres above sea level, it lies mainly in a north-south direction, following the River Meschio, and is halfway between Venice and Cortina d'Ampezzo, high in the Italian dolomites. Thanks to its geographical position the city has been a destination since ancient times, used for conquests, transits, settlements and architecture, and is still a much used direct route from Venice to Austria. The extraordinary beauty of the landscape, the beautiful traditional centre and the local gastronomy make this an ideal place to visit.

Vittorio Veneto

History

The first inhabitants of the area were the Paleoveneti, an ancient Indo-European population present on the northern Adriatic coasts from 1200 BC. Evidence of early settlements, documented by coins, tombs and tombstones, dates back to the Roman conquest and subsequent Lombard rule.

Today's city was born in 1866 from the fusion of two ancient municipalities: Serravalle, the centre rich in trade and artisanal activities, and Ceneda, a former political and administrative town. A new urban centre was built, replete with Umbertine buildings. The re-naming of the municipality to Vittorio Veneto came from the fierce battle that took place from 24 October-3 November 1918, resulting in the end of the First World War just one week later. The city took the name Vittorio Veneto on July 22, 1923 and was awarded the Gold Medal for Military Valour for the acts of many of its partisans who assisted in bringing the conflict to a successful completion.

Early artisanal activities lead us to Lanificio Bottoli, just one of the six woollen mills that were originally set up in the area. This highly successful company was founded in 1861 for the production of woollen blankets and cloths and, having survived the crippling crisis following the Second World War, it changed production to the manufacture of patterned fabrics.

Lanificio Bottoli is now one of the best-known Italian fabric companies, producing 2,500 metres of fabric each day. Their process includes the collection and selection of native wool using the natural colours of Merino sheep, which has led to a surge in Italian sheep farming.

Feasts and Events

Ancient Festival of San Tiziano – January 16

Traditional festival with religious and sporting events (a march on the day of the Epiphany; running a relay from Oderzo to Vittorio Veneto, which is a re-enactment of the miraculous journey made by the saint's remains), amusement park, cultural events, children's bonfire.

The Foghi of Santa Augusta – midnight, August 21

A great firework display that has attracted thousands of spectators for years, filling the historic centre of Serravalle.

National Bird Market Show – Aug 15

This centuries-old exhibition takes place every August 15th with aviary birds, poultry, and a singing competition conducted between the categories of birds, presentation of companion dogs, demonstrations of dog agility and falconry. The event takes place in the central area of Serravalle.

National String Reviews and Biennial National Violin Competition – end of September

A national event, started in 1962, dedicated to bowed instruments, which brings young musicians from all over Italy to Vittorio Veneto. It's a launching pad for those who are now established musicians in the international arena. Organised by the Municipality of Vittorio Veneto.

Vittorio Veneto Film Festival – April

International film festival for children, which combines ingenuity and culture. In fact, film watching is accompanied by participation in collateral activities such as meetings with the directors, workshops, adjudication and other initiatives. Organised by the Cultural Association.

National Palio of Barrels – A summer festival

The Palio delle Botti is a national event in which all the member municipalities who want to meet and challenge each other are invited to participate, rolling and pushing 500 litre barrels through the streets of the city.

<u>Wines in Loggia – Held in early May</u>

As part of the Spring Exhibitions of Prosecco: tastings guided by sommeliers, live music and themed gastronomic evenings. Organised by the Pro Loco Vittorio Veneto.

<u>Mediaeval Days: The Children's Castle and the Palio dei Borghi and Contrade – last week of May</u>

Historical re-enactment, archery shows, demonstrations with birds of prey, arts and crafts, duels at the Castrum of Serravalle, reconstructions of a mediaeval camp, conferences and cultural events.

<u>Market Day</u>

A market is held weekly on Monday mornings.

Places of Interest

Allow plenty of time for your visit as there is so much to see in Vittorio Veneto. It's a characterful city with a wonderful distinguished legacy. There are some eye-catching mediaeval buildings and historic squares where you can absorb the history, stopping occasionally for the obligatory Italian coffee or gelato.

Wander along the side of the River Meschio or admire the illustrious works of art, including a Titian, in the city's many churches. The area has many nature walks too.

There's a direct train from Venice, which takes just under 1.5 hours, or plenty of on-street meter parking if you're in a car; traffic is fairly easy to negotiate and is not too demanding.

Piazza Flaminio

I would recommend starting your tour in Serravalle. The heart of Serravalle is the Piazza Flaminio, the original market square, paved with pink Istrian stones. Built according to Renaissance urban planning, it is surrounded by elegant facades of buildings, arranged on three sides of the square, including the exquisitely ornate façade of the Museum of the Cenedese. On the fourth side you can see the River Meschio and the bridge that crosses it by the side of the Cathedral Church of Santa Maria Nuova.

The huge bulk of the Church of Santa Maria Nuova, with its soaring façade, is visible almost entirely only from Piazza Flaminio. Erected in the second half of the 18th century in place of a pre-existing Romanesque church, its slightly austere exterior was designed in neoclassical style by the Tolmezzo architect Schiavi. The church is replete with fascinating, precious works of art, its most important being the large original altarpiece painted by Titian between 1542 and 1547, depicting the Madonna with Child and Saints Andrew and Peter. The walls of the presbytery also house two panels painted by Francesco da Milano, whilst the ceiling displays a work by Gian

Battista Canal (1743-1825), grandson of Canaletto. It also houses a 19th century organ, built by Agostino and Antonio Callido, which is of great value and often used for classical music concerts. The bell tower stands in an isolated position on the north-west side of the cathedral and was built in 1562 on the remains of an ancient tower.

Titian found in Santa Maria Nuova

Leaving the Duomo (cathedral) through the side door, you will enter Via Casoni in the ancient Tiera district, where former merchants' houses jostle for position down the quaint old street. At the end of Via Casoni, cross the small bridge of the 'Beccaria', which gives a view of the Meschet hydraulic works that divide the riverbed into three different courses in case of flood and leads to the Scuola dei Battuti building on the left: an imposing quadrangular structure, used as a civil hospital for a long time and now destined for other use pending a renovation project (part of the complex currently houses a high school).

Walking past the school along Via Pietro Paietta, you will arrive in Piazzetta Tiziano Vecellio. To the south (left), the square is formed by the Church of San Lorenzo dei Battuti (annexed to the old school) and flanked by the San Lorenzo gate, part of the circle of walls erected by the Caminesi to defend Serravalle in the early decades of the 13th century. To the north you can see another of the rich houses of Serravalle, Palazzo Sarcinelli, home to Titian's daughter, Lavinia, who married Cornelio Sarcinelli, and whose delicate features can be admired in portraits by the great painter.

Vittorio Veneto

Through the arch of Porta di San Lorenzo, the road changes its name to the Via Cavour.

Meanwhile, turning back onto Via Martiri della Libertà, parallel to Via Casoni and the Meschio, there is the backdrop of splendid and ancient Serravalle residences, almost all built with a large hall on the main floor, and a balcony for the orchestra and guests. The street is flanked by a long and continuous portico typical of the time, which brings out the wall surfaces of the fronts of the buildings, with mullioned windows and balconies which, at one time, would have been entirely frescoed.

The northern tip of the defensive bulwark of Serravalle is Porta Cadore. Here, on the east of the river, is the Church of Santa Giustina, which hosts the Mausoleum of Rizzardo VI da Camino, an important Lombard knight.

The stand out for this church is that it preserves the most extraordinary example of a Gothic sarcophagus, beautifully produced by Venetian masons and possibly the best preserved in the country. This mausoleum was commissioned by Verde della Scala sometime between 1336 and 1340 as a tribute to her husband, Rizzardo VI da Camino. The grandiose sepulchre, which is the only work of the Lombardian family left in Italy, was originally located in the centre of the church and was supported by six rather than the current four figures of praying warriors, which are from an even earlier period.

The 14th century Church of San Lorenzo dei Battuti is entirely frescoed inside with episodes from the life of San Marco and San Lorenzo. The gothic decoration, carried out between 1429 and 1446 by a local artist, represents one of the best-preserved pictorial complexes in the Veneto region, despite the ravages of time and its multiple uses.

Found in Serravalle a little way out from the main square, the Church of San Giovanni Battista was built in a Romanesque-Gothic form in 1357 and modernised in Renaissance style, with the later addition of a portal and a rose window. The colourful Gothic-style interior is embellished with a multitude of frescoes by artists such as Francesco da Milano, Jacobello del Fiore, Francesco Frigimelica, Jacopo da Valenza and Antonio Zago. The richness of the internal decoration and the beauty of the architectural structure make this building a very valuable art monument.

Frescoes at San Giovanni

The Sanctuary of Santa Augusta (patron saint of Serravalle) has always drawn pilgrims and visitors alike and houses the mortal remains of Santa Augusta who, legend says, accompanies the visitor along the terraced path, built on the slopes of Mount Marcantone. According to legend, Augusta, daughter of the barbarian King Matrucco, used to bring bread to the poor, against the wishes of her father. One day, her father surprised her as she descended from the castle to the village below. She confidently opened the mantle that contained the charitable offering and the loaves turned into flowers. Along the footpath that leads to the sanctuary, a shrine and worn stone indicates the place where the miracle is purported to have occurred.

Sant'Andrea di Bigonzo

Whilst strolling through the city, heading south towards Ceneda on the left is a majestic tree-lined avenue that leads to the oldest and most beautiful architectural monument of the diocese: the Church of Sant'Andrea di Bigonzo, with its 25 frescoes, all from the 15th and 16th centuries. Its humble appearance at the fork in the road belies the grandeur found inside. Mentioned in 13th century historical documents, the interior space houses frescoes and important works of art from a variety of local artists: Marco and Cesare Vecellio, Francesco da Milano, Francesco Frigimelica, Antonello da Serravalle and Palma the Younger.

On the Piazza Giovanni Paolo 1 you will find a large square situated in front of the major buildings of old Ceneda: the Loggia, which houses the Battle of Vittorio Veneto Museum; the Cathedral; and the Episcopal Seminary, founded in 1587 but altered in the mid-20th century after being repurposed to house convalescing soldiers from the Great War. The Castello San Martino can also be seen in the hills above the square.

Museo della Battaglia

The Museo della Battaglia (Museum of the Battle) was the initiative of Luigi Marson, whose first find was a rosary belonging to a Hungarian soldier, discovered on the banks of the Piave. This started the passion of a lifetime as he sought to reconstruct the events of the war in which he participated through objects and documents. In 1936, his first public exhibition took place; he subsequently donated the war memorabilia to the city of Vittorio Veneto.

The Museo della Battaglia

The Cathedral of the Blessed Virgin Mary of the Assumption is on the site of an early 4th-century place of worship but has suffered several rebuilds and replacements due to its precarious condition. The current church, designed by Ottavio Scotti, was built during the 18th century.

The building is full of gilding, frescoes and important works of art, commensurate with its stature as a cathedral church. Of special note is the oil painting by Bonifacio da Verona (c. 1487-1553) containing the figures of San Giovanni Battista, San Nicolò Vescovo and the martyr San Vito. There are two paintings by Palma il Giovane (1548-1628), one above the entrance whilst the other can be seen on the fourth altar of the left aisle. Another altarpiece is a painting depicting the Ascension by Leandro Da Ponte (1557-1662).

Blessed Virgin Mary of the Assumption

Visible from Piazza Papa Giovanni Paolo I, located high on a hillside, the Castello San Martino is the residence of the Bishop of the diocese. It was originally built in Roman times but as with many fortresses in this area, it suffered from targeted Hungarian attack requiring rebuilding, which was completed between 1420 and 1430. It is located at 198 metres above sea level in a peaceful, ambient setting among greenery and lush trees and is a good starting point for many of the nature trails in the hills around the city.

Castle San Martino

The hills of Vittorio Veneto have countless paths that wander up through lush vegetation and lead to many of the shrines and sanctuaries that dominate the city from above, or pass by the Croce del Monte Altare, a 12-metre-high cross which is found 450 metres above sea level.

Notable Locals

Alessandro Tandura (1893-1937) was a member of the illustrious Arditi, a lieutenant of the XX Assault Department and the world's first paratrooper. In August 1918, he launched into the sky in severe weather conditions, with lightning, thunder and torrential rain. The first 'flight' didn't go according to plan: some of this was due to the adverse weather but some was also due to the nature of the drop. The plane, a Savoy Pomilio, was piloted by the Canadian flier, Major Baker, and Alessandro was curled up under the cockpit in a small housing. The observer pilot released the lever when it was supposed to be over the drop zone but calculation was done by eye and time in the air, which led to the paratrooper being dropped into the garden of the parish priest of San Martino di Colle Umberto instead of the Meadows of Savassa where he was supposed to land.

Tandura started gathering information on the enemy units in the area. Assisted by his girlfriend and his sister, he organised sabotage actions on ammunition depots and other strategic positions. During his mission he was twice taken prisoner and managed to escape both times.

WINERIES

This area is at the north of the Prosecco DOCG area and, unlike Valdobbiadene, does not have a huge selection of wineries. Although fewer in number, they still offer something different to the visitor and can be combined with a visit to the centre of Vittorio Veneto.

BELLENDA
Via Gaetano Giardino, 90 31029 Vittorio Veneto Loc. Carpesica TV, Italia
+390438920025
info@bellenda.it | www.bellenda.it

Wine tastings, accommodation, retail sales, winery & vineyard visits
Production between 100,000 and 500,000 bottles

Bellenda winery shop

I've visited this modern, elegant environment a couple of times. The entrance is directly into the sales area, which has some different products on offer, but the outstanding thing about Bellenda is they have really thought about how to differentiate their tastings for visitors. Alongside the more usual cellar visit and Prosecco tasting they offer food plates, picnics or, for the adventurous, a 2.5-hour motorbike and sidecar experience around the vineyards and surroundings. The Relais-style accommodation is co-located with the winery; it is small and exclusive, with top quality furnishings and set in a beautiful environment.

LE VIGNE DI ALICE
Via della Chiesa, 20, Carpesica, Vittorio Veneto, TV, Italia
+390438920818
cinzia@levignedialice.it | www.levignedialice.it

Wine tasting, accommodation, retail sales and winery visits
Production up to 150,000 bottles

CANTINA DI CONEGLIANO E VITTORIO VENETO
Via del Campardo, 3, Vittorio Veneto, TV, Italia
Vittorio Veneto +390438500209 Conegliano +39043822268
info@cantinavittorio.it, info@cantinadiconegliano.it |
www.cantinavittorio.it

Wine tasting, retail sales, winery visits
Production up to 150,000 bottles

CENETAE Az. Agr. dell'Ist. Diocesano per il Sost.nto del Clero
via Jacopo Stella, 34 Vittorio Veneto
+390438552043 | +390438949399
commerciale@cenetae.it | www.cenetae.it

Open to the public, a working farm set up for the welfare of the

clergy of Vittorio and Conegliano
Production up to 150,000 bottles

LA VIGNA DI SARAH

Via del Bersagliere, 30/a, Vittorio Veneto, TV, Italia
+393406003442
info@lavignadisarah.it | www.lavignadisarah.it

Wine tasting, accommodation, retail sales and winery visits
Production between 100,000 and 500,000 bottles

A grand sweeping road leads up to this hilltop location where a
pretty, covered outside area sits aside a farmhouse building. Run by
Sarah and now entirely organic, she differentiates by offering
cookery classes and accommodation. The quaint, compact, quirky
accommodation is set in human-sized barrels, fully furnished
complete with ensuite facilities. Their unique selling point is
harvesting the grapes at night-time during cooler temperatures.

La Vigna di Sarah

BARBARA ROMANI FACCO WINERY
Via Manzana, 46, Formeniga, Vittorio Veneto
barbararomanifacco@gmail.com

Open to the public but no further information given

TONON Vini srl
Via Carpesica, 1, Carpesica, Vittorio Veneto, TV, Italia
+390438920004 | +390438920014
info@vinitonon.com | www.vinitonon.com

Wine tastings, retail sales, winery visits
Production up to 150,000 bottles

9. TARZO

Number of inhabitants: 4,336
Altitude: 267
Area km2: 23.91
Patron Saint: Purification of the Virgin Mary – Feb 2; Arfanta –
Saint Bartholomew – third week of August

Tarzo is located around 60 km north of Venice. This area is a
popular holiday destination due to its mild winter and cool summer
climates. Famous for its house murals, Tarzo starts from the
monument of Piazza IV Novembre and continues along the narrow
streets of the town. Several works of art, some dedicated to
emigration, others to ancient crafts and popular traditions, are
visible dotted around on the ancient buildings of the town streets.
These traditional frescoes are interspersed with up-to-date murals
by local artists and the two different styles work well together for a
perfect visual display.

Tarzo

History

Evidence of a human presence purporting to be from between the Neolithic and Bronze Ages has been found in the area, proving the existence of a pile-dwelling settlement. Further into the Alpine Region is a UNESCO World Heritage Site of pile dwellings dating back to between 5000-50 BC. These ancient inhabitants, of Venetian and Celtic lineage, present since the 2nd millennium BC, were finally absorbed into the Roman Empire as early as the 2nd century BC.

Feasts

Festa della Candelora (Candle festival), in Tarzo

This takes place in the last week of January and the first week of February. The programme includes a parade of floats, a lottery and a Carnival drawing competition in collaboration with the local lower secondary school.

Panevin (Bonfire festival)

Tradition has it that on the evening of 5th January, the eve of Epiphany, the 'vecia', an ancient figure, is burnt on a huge 'panevin' (bonfire). It's a characteristic feature throughout the Veneto region and in the province of Treviso in particular. People from the neighbouring villages gather around it to eat 'pinza' (a tasty fragrant cake made of polenta, sultanas and fennel seeds) and drink 'vin brulè' (mulled wine with cloves, cinnamon and sometimes apples). Panevin takes place in all the hamlets of Tarzo and some of the surrounding municipalities.

Festa della Castagna di Colmaggiore e delle colline tarzesi (Chestnut festival in Colmaggiore and the hills of Tarzo)

Held during the first three weeks of October, the festival revolves around promoting local chestnuts known as 'marroni'. The culinary part also includes grilled specialities and typical dishes such as 'polenta e mus' (cornmeal porridge with donkey meat), venison and meat on the spit.

Spirito degli Antichi Sapori (Spirit of Ancient Flavours)

The market exhibition of arts and crafts is organised by the PRO.G.E.T.T.O. association. Stalls exhibit local products and crafts, with tastings of typical specialities as well as cheese-making, preparation of cured cold cuts, and several other attractions connected with ancient farming traditions.

Market

A weekly market is held on Wednesday mornings.

Places of Interest

Giardino Museo Bonsai della Serenità (Bonsai Garden Museum of Serenity)

At the back of the house of Antonio Dal Col is the Bonsai Garden Museum of Serenity. The botanical garden can be visited every day between 10 am -12 noon and 2.30-7 pm. See the immense collection of bonsai, many of which have won Japanese awards.

Livelet Educational Archaeological Park

The Livelet Educational Archaeological Park is located on the western shore of Lake Lago and contains the reconstructed pile dwelling village and other educational activities.

The nature walks through the Parco dei Laghi (Park of the Lakes) of Revine and Tarzo are beautiful, serene walks, interspersed with overgrown reeds and scented waterlilies. There are several walking trails of between 4-5 km joined by a wooden bridge with an observation tower, and also one of the first natural/digital routes in augmented reality: Parco locale dei Laghi (Local Park of the Lakes).

Livelet Educational Archaeological Park
(photograph courtesy of Sui Colle)

Lago di Lago

WINERIES

ANDREA DA PONTE
Via I Maggio, 1, Corbanese, Tarzo, TV, Italia
+390438933011 | +390438933874
info@daponte.it | www.daponte.it

Wine tastings, retail sales
Production up to 150,000 bottles

SOCIETA AGRICOLA PRAPIAN SRL
Via Arfanta, Località Prapian di Tarzo Tv, Italia
+390499385023 | +390499386075
mail@sacchettovini.it | www.prapianvini.it

Wine tastings, winery visits, vineyard visits
Production up to 150,000 bottles
Totally organic

VINI SARA MENEGUZ (Az. Agr. MENEGUZ CESARE)
via Ghettei 13, 31020 Corbanese di Tarzo, TV, Italia
+393389454185
comerciale@vinimeneguzsara.it | www.vinimeneguzsara.it

Wine tasting, retail sales, vineyard visits
Production up to 150,000 bottles

10. REFRONTOLO

Number of inhabitants: 1,702
Altitude: 216 (varies)
Area km²: 13.04
Patron Saint: Santa Margherita – Jul 20

Refrontolo is situated on a hill overlooking the Piave river and along the valley of Crevada, another great destination for a picturesque walk. The name Refrontolo is an adaptation of the Latin 'Ronco' (deforested, undiscovered place) and 'Frontulo', a topographical feature that refers to a wooded area; together, the words mean a village among wooded hills.

Refrontolo

Refrontolo offers visitors a great selection of places to eat: rural cottages (where you can eat the produce of nearby farms), rustic taverns and restaurants. The Refrontolo and San Pietro areas are one of the hotspots of the wine region, boasting 14 wineries and 1 mobile bottling machine. The vineyards produce local wines including Prosecco, Marzemino, Verdiso and Manzoni. The history of the area is inextricably linked with the history of wine production. The wine produced in the areas of Refrontolo, Conegliano and surroundings is discussed in the historical document of 6th November 1431, in which the Doge della Serenissima requests the Podestà of Conegliano, Stefano Erizzo, to send him the usual load of good Feletto wine.

Refrontolo

History

The ancient territory of Refrontolo is documented as early as 1075. This document refers to a tithe paid to the monastery of Saints Candido and Corbiniano of Innichen, and the abbot, Bishop of Freising. The village is referred to in several ways: Roncum Frontulum, Ronco Frontulo, Roncofrontolo in 1128, and Refrontali in 1266. The current name, Refrontolo, starts to appear in documents from 1540.

In the 18th century, there was a decisive oenological decline. In 1709, a heavy frost caused almost all the vines to die. They were replaced with more rustic and less valuable vines with a production of sour wine, such as Raboso, which diluted the quality. The cultivation and improvement in wine-growing techniques was assisted by the institution of the Academy of Agriculture and the appearance of the first wine school in neighbouring Conegliano.

In Refrontolo, and in a few other neighbouring areas, Marzemino Nero has been cultivated and the grapes dried for the production of an excellent passito that, in 1978, entered the Refrontolo wine exhibition as a typical product and obtained the coveted DOC under the name 'Refrontolo Passito'. A sweet heavy wine, almost port-like, can be found in the area, in white and red varieties.

Places of Interest

Molinetta della Croda

Refrontolo is also known for the enchanting 17th century Molinetta della Croda waterwheel, which can be found in a picturesque part of the Lierza valley on the small country road between Cison and Solighetto. The natural waterfall provided the perfect conditions for modest families of millers to trade.

Unfortunately, devastating floods in 1941 and 1953 proved too much for the impoverished millers and the mill was eventually abandoned after the last flood in 1953. More recently, the mill has been restored and is once more functional. Its quiet, natural beauty makes it a pleasant stop-off point for a picnic. For those of us who want the perfect photo, this is an excellent stop on the tour and you can't fail to fall in love with its picturesque tranquil beauty.

WINERIES

TOFFOLI SOC. AGR. S.S.
Via Liberazione, 26, Refrontolo, TV, Italia
+394380978204
toffoli@proseccotoffoli.it | www.proseccotoffoli.it

Wine tasting, retail sales, sale of local products, winery visits, vineyard visits
Production between 100,000 and 500,000 bottles

Toffoli winery

A perfect display of a full range of Prosecco, local reds/whites and a very warm welcome!

If you only have the opportunity to visit one winery in the region, this is the one I'd recommend. Definitely in my top three of the whole area. I've visited many times and directed many visitors here and they have all reported the same fabulous experience.

The winery is run by the Toffoli family, inherited from parents Vincenzo and Maria, and their legacy is very much in evidence around the winery and also on the bottles of extremely drinkable Prosecco. Your host will invariably be Sante Toffoli, proficient in English, his softly spoken manner and pleasant ambience making everyone feel at ease and gaining quick interest in the production process. Expect to see him in his sleeveless pullover as the temperature varies between the tasting room and the inside of the winery with its multitude of cold steel tanks.

Toffoli products

The winery is in the most picturesque setting: rolling hills, tiny hamlets and few people around. The Toffoli winery is around 20 hectares and production is based on the local vines, with some co-opted from local farmers whilst being strictly monitored by Luciano to ensure the required quality is achieved. They regularly participate in shows and European events, claiming many awards.

Elegant glass to serve Prosecco

Sante's tasting will be one of the longer ones, so sit and enjoy the atmosphere as he produces bottle after bottle of the sparkling stuff, interspersed with light bites of delectable local cheese on small bread rounds. His Proseccos are amazing, a firm favourite for me and my tasting events. They range from a Brut Zero and an organic Prosecco all the way through the range to the sweeter, 'dry'

Prosecco. When you've had your fill of those, he will produce some beautiful, delicate local white wine, Verdiso, and some robust and full structured red wines. You'll lose count. If you're still game, there's more. Refrontolo is known for its passito and the Toffoli winery produces three different varieties. Don't be afraid to try one. You'll find it hard to leave without purchasing your favourite – the trouble is, which one?

Outside Toffoli winery

ASTORIA VINI
Via Crevada 31020 Refrontolo, Italia
+39 04236699
info@astoria.it | www.astoria.it

Wine tastings, retail sales, winery & vineyard visits
Production listed as between 100,000 and 500,000 bottles

I called without an appointment one afternoon. The winery is fronted by a shop-type environment with a fabulous display of different wines: red, white and Prosecco. A larger business, they have a distributor of Prosecco in the UK; I emailed to find out who but unfortunately never got a reply. Still fab Prosecco though.

CANTINA BERNARDI
Via Colvendrame, 25, Refrontolo, TV, Italia
+390438894153 | +390438894542
bernardi@cantinabernardi.it | www.cantinabernardi.it

Wine tastings, retail sales
Production up to 150,000 bottles

A small, award-winning winery, established on the road to Refrontolo. This was one of my earlier visits and I called without an appointment. They were still able to provide a tasting of their superb Prosecco.

Cantina Bernardi

COL SALIZ DI FAGANELLO ANTONIO Az. Agr.
Via Colvendrame, 48/b, Refrontolo, TV, Italia
+390438894026 | +390438978129
info@colsaliz.it | www.colsaliz.it

Wine tastings available Monday-Friday. Also retail sales
No further information is available

COLVENDRA

Via Liberazione, 39, Refrontolo, TV, Italia

+390438894265 | +390438894626

info@colvendra.it | www.colvendra.it

Wine tastings, retail sales

Production up to 150,000 bottles

Colvendra was established in 1924 and is still run by the same family. It has a wide range of Prosecco and local red and white wines.

AI RORE

Via Patrioti, 2, 31020 Refrontolo TV

+390438894241

airore-destefani@libero.it | airore.it

Production up to 150,000 bottles

Not known if this is open to the public

11. SAN PIETRO DI FELETTO

Number of inhabitants: 5,219
Altitude: 221m
Area km^2: 19.26
Patron Saint: Saint Peter the Apostle – Jun 29

San Pietro di Feletto is a municipality of slightly over 5,000 inhabitants that stands on the hills, embroidered by a multitude of vineyards, to the northwest of Conegliano. From its hills, the view extends to the south to Conegliano, to the west on the gentle curve of Montello and to the north on the belt of the Treviso Prealps. The territory, dotted with rows of vines that are tinged with emerald green in spring and yellow-gold in autumn, has numerous testimonies of its mediaeval past, such as Borgo Anese, a charming rural community, and the Antica Pieve (ancient church) with its excellently preserved frescoes.

View from Piave San Pietro di Feletto

The name Feletto derives from the Latin 'felix-icis', a place where ferns abound. The area was once covered by woods rich in ferns and tall trees: beech, alder, maple and birch, some of which were used for maintaining the Venetian sailing fleet. However, there was also no shortage of land rich in olive and vine plantations, to the point that even the Doge of Venice, Francesco Foscari mentioned the "good wine of Feletto" in a 1431 epistle.

View from Piave San Pietro di Feletto

History

San Pietro di Feletto is probably one of the oldest parishes in the entire territory of the ancient Diocese of Ceneda. The history of this territory, of a wine-growing vocation, begins with Christianity around the 4th-5th centuries, when the church dedicated to San Pietro Apostolo was erected, most likely on the foundations of a previous pagan temple. In the second half of the 17th century, a Camaldolese hermitage was built on the Capriolo hill and used as a municipal seat. The history of the hermitage began in 1670 when the Venetian patrician, Alvise Canal, bequeathed a hill to the hermit monks of San Romualdo.

Feasts

Hill Wines Exhibition

This takes place in the old hermitage in Rua di Feletto, organised by the Pro Loco of San Pietro di Feletto and included in the circuit of Spring Prosecco exhibitions. You can taste the wine production of the Altamarca Trevigiana, from Prosecco Superiore DOCG of Conegliano Valdobbiadene to the Colli di Conegliano DOCG wines. The exhibition is very well attended by local producers and much appreciated by the public.

Panevin

Traditional bonfire on the evening of January 5th in the hamlets of Rua, Santa Maria, San Pietro Vecchio, San Michele and Bagnolo. The flame symbolizes hope for the new year by burning the negative things of the past year, represented by the 'vecia' placed above the woodpile. The direction of the smoke will indicate whether it will be a good or bad year.

Places of Interest

Latteria Perenzin

I can't discuss San Pietro di Feletto without making mention of the Latteria Perenzin. The company specialises in cheese making and has an adjoining café where you can sample the delights of their four generations of expert production of both goat's milk cheese and a very wide range of organic and conventional cow and buffalo Veneto cheeses.

Select your cheese or something from the wide range of cooked meats – not the easiest of things to do with all the wonderful but very different, unrecognisable cheeses on offer – and wash the plate down with the obligatory glass of Prosecco. Why not!

Perenzin Latteria

Perenzin Latteria srl., Via Cervano, 85 – loc, Bagnolo. 31020 San Pietro di Feletto. Tel: +39 0438 21355. Email: info@perenzin.com

The Pieve di San Pietro

If you only visit one of the plethora of churches listed on these pages, this should be the one, not only for the church but also its dominant, perfectly elevated position and far-reaching views. It's quite exquisite and has a rare calmness surrounding it.

The Pieve di San Pietro, dating back to the 11th century, is one of the oldest and most precious churches in the area. It is thought it was used as a meeting place in the 7th and 8th centuries and that the original structure was built over the ruins of a pagan temple. The church is accessed by a central staircase leading to a churchyard covered by a large mediaeval porch.

As well as a meeting place, the original church was used for baptisms. In fact, the Pieve was the only church to have a baptismal font inside when it was built.

Pieve di San Pietro

Walk around the entrance porch to see several notable and detailed frescoes: St Antony Abbot, the Virgin with Child, and the Virgin with Saints, important for a very rare detail, that of the infant Jesus sucking milk from a bladder, with which it is thought the painter refers to the customs of the poor families of that time. You'll also see the sacrifice of Cain and Abel and the notable 14th century Christ of Sunday, a rare image, surrounded by the numerous tools once used in the fields. It's a symbol of popular religious culture of the late Middle Ages, aimed at reminding the people of the obligation of rest and sanctification on Sunday. The painting is interesting and informative because it gives a pictorial image of tools used in those times and the type of work undertaken. These types of ancient frescoes are quite rare and it is thought there are less than a dozen throughout Europe.

Fresco Pieve di San Pietro

The inside of the church is colourful, eye-catching and completely awe-inspiring as it is almost completely covered in frescoes, artist unknown. Entering the church, you will see the baptismal font, with a cross-shaped ceiling decorated with a cycle of frescoes dating back to the 15th century, depicting episodes from the life of San Sebastiano.

The walls of the central nave are frescoed with works showing hints of its Byzantine legacy, ranging from the 13th to the 15th centuries. On the right wall is the Cycle of Creed, a singular example of the 'Bible of the Poor', a pictorial religious demonstration designed to be understood even by those who could not read. Opening hours are only guaranteed on Sundays and public holidays between 3-7pm.

It's hard to believe that all these frescoes were hidden under a heavy coat of white paint and only 'rediscovered' at the end of the 1800s. Delicate restoration has brought the original artwork back to life whilst more recent renovation has been carried out to consolidate the structures from the after-effects of the earthquake of 1873.

The separate bell tower, which rises, isolated, with a 16th century spire, is in Romanesque style modelled on that of Aquileia.

There's a nature trail that touches the churches of San Pietro and Santa Maria, develops along the route carved out by the Crevada stream, and flows through a picturesque valley. Along the way there are several places of note, in particular the sites of the 'Val Trippera' ford and the ruin of Molino Crevada. The numerous springs, the 'Landri' and 'Landron' caves are typical features in this area, and have given rise to other underground caves, bores and sinkholes typical of karst (soluble rock such as limestone) rock structures.

WINERIES

Az Agr SAN GIUSEPPE

Via Po, 10/a, Crevada, San Pietro di Feletto, TV, Italia
+39 0438 450526 | +39 0438 651664
vini.sangiuseppe@libero.it | www.aziendaagricolasangiuseppe.it

Wine tastings, retail sales, winery & vineyard visits
Production between 100,000 and 500,000 bottles

San Giuseppe Prosecco

A short visit on one of my earlier trips. They are one of the few wineries that produce a Tranquillo DOCG and I enjoyed that and the Brut Prosecco.

BEPIN DE ETO - Soc. Agr. di Ceschin Ettore s.s.
Via Colle, 32/a, Borgo Colle, San Pietro di Feletto, TV, Italia
+390438486877 | +390438787854
info@bepindeeto.it | www.bepindeeto.it

Retail sales, winery visits
Production between 500,000 and 1,000,000 bottles

DE RIZ Az. Agr.
via Pianale 72/A San Pietro di Feletto
+390438784115
info@proseccoderiz.it | www.proseccoderiz.it

Wine tastings, retail sales, winery & vineyard visits
Production up to 150,000 bottles

Outside tasting at De Riz

I managed a short visit to this winery, accompanied by my nieces.

It's at the top of the area, a simple building but with tasting options under the natural vine terrace, accompanied by their wonderful Prosecco, of course, along with other local wines. Speak to Pamela.

CANTINA I BAMBOI sas
Via Brandolini, 13, San Pietro di Feletto, TV, Italia
+390438787038
ibamboi@tmn.it | www.ibamboi.it

Wine tastings, retail sales & winery visits
Production up to 150,000 bottles

SOC. AGR. CASTELLALTA S.S.
Via Castella, 17/A loc. Rua di Feletto
+393477806498
info@castellalta.it | www.castellalta.it

Wine tasting, retail sales
Production up to 150,000 bottles

IL COLLE 1978
Via Colle, 15, 31020 San Pietro di Feletto
+390438486926 | +390438787958
info@proseccoilcolle.it | www.proseccoilcolle.it

Wine tastings, retail sales & winery visits
Production over 1,000,000 bottles

I've been to Il Colle several times. It's a larger organisation, so a professional welcome and a slicker delivery – not that I have a problem with that! Several options on tastings are available. They have a large tasting room and visits to the production area are also possible. The big problem with this winery is knowing what to taste and then what to purchase – all their Prosecco is fabulous!

Il Colle Prosecco

SANFELETTO srl
Via Borgo Antiga, 39, Borgo Antiga, San Pietro di Feletto, TV, Italia
+390438486832 | +390438787890
sanfeletto@sanfeletto.it | www.sanfeletto.it

Wine tastings, retail sales & winery visits

SOC AGR MORET s.s. di MORET RENZO e C. (LA SVOLTA)
via Condel 5, San Pietro di Feletto
0438784251
info@proseccolasvolta.it | www.proseccolasvolta.it

Wine tastings, retail sales, winery & vineyard visits
Production up to 150,000 bottles

LE MANZANE

Via Maset, 47/b, Casotto, San Pietro di Feletto, TV, Italia
+390438486606
info@lemanzane.it | www.lemanzane.com

Wine tastings, retail sales, winery & vineyard visits
Production over 1,000,000 bottles

MANI SAGGE

Via Manzana, 46, Manzana, 31020 San Pietro di Feletto, TV, Italia
info@manisagge.com | www.manisagge.com

Wine tastings, retail sales & vineyard visits
Production up to 150,000 bottles

Mani Sagge food plate

We arrived at this recently renovated winery in the middle of an uncharacteristic August hailstorm, which unfortunately dictated the view out of the massive picture window of the tasting room. Smaller Prosecco wineries have a legacy steeped in family. Our host, Marco, explained how his grandfather enjoyed seeing his development of the building and winery to include accommodation. The Prosecco was plentiful and accompanied by a plate piled with meats and cheeses for our tasting session. The winery produces around 30,000 bottles and Marco has real passion and a clear perspective of what his tastings should offer in terms of experiences.

MASCHIO BENIAMINO srl
Via San Michele, 70, San Pietro di Feletto, TV, Italia
+390438450023 | +39043860034
info@beniaminomaschio.it | www.beniaminomaschio.it

Open to the public, no further info known

MORET VINI
Via Condel, 2A San Pietro di Feletto
+393400839642
info@moretvini.it | moretvini.it

Wine tastings, retail sales, sale of local food products, winery & vineyard visits
Production up to 150,000 bottles

SANFELETTO srl
Via Borgo Antiga, 39, Borgo Antiga, San Pietro di Feletto, TV, Italia
+390438486832 | +390438787890
sanfeletto@sanfeletto.it | www.sanfeletto.it

Wine tastings, retail sales & winery visits

SOMMARIVA Soc. Agr. PALAZZO ROSSO S.S.
Via Luciani Albino, 16/a, Santa Maria, San Pietro di Feletto, TV,
Italia
+390438784316
info@sommariva-vini.it | www.sommariva-vini.it

Wine tastings, retail sales, winery & vineyard visits
Production of between 100,000 and 500,000 bottles

VETTORI Az. Agr. di VETTORI ARTURO
Via Borgo America, 26, Borgo America, San Pietro di Feletto, TV,
Italia
+39043834812 | +39043834812
info@vinivettori.it | www.vinivettori.it

Wine tastings and winery visits
Up to 150,000 bottles

12. CISON DI VALMARINO

Number of inhabitants: 2,632
Altitude: 261m
Area km²: 28.81
Patron Saint: St John the Baptist – June 24

Located near the northern border of the March of Treviso, Cison di Valmarino has many historical and artistic attractions: the archpriest's church of Santa Maria, numerous roadside shrines, Brandolini Castle, the Temple of the Madonna delle Grazie, the Vintage Radio Museum, Tovena parish church with its priceless Callido organ, the brand-new Religious Art Museum, and the '100-Day Road' that elevates from the valley bottom to the San Boldo.

Cison di Valmarino

Steeped in tradition and rural living, the municipality of Cison di Valmarino is further characterised by small industry and artisan businesses rooted in the territory for decades.

The most popular and well-known building in the municipality is the splendid mediaeval castle, which stands in an imposing position on the hill about a hundred metres from the centre. In the past it was the centre of political power and a point of reference for the entire area. Within its walls visitors can relive the stories of battles and duels, of ladies and knights.

Looking down from its imposing bastions, the panoramic view incorporates the small-town centre of Cison with its compact yet elegant square, the theatre La Loggia, once the seat of the county court, the fields and the landscape of the surrounding hills, which are perfect for trekking and horse riding. The mild climate and strategic location, particularly sheltered in a sunny amphitheatre formed by the surrounding hills, make Cison di Valmarino a popular tourist destination throughout the year.

The pace is not hurried here and the landscape boasts a lifestyle that has changed little for centuries.

The imposing Castelbrando

History

The town of Cison suffered an economic crisis between the wars when many of the town's inhabitants left to seek work in the cities. Attempts were made to stop the outflow of young people and stimulate the local economy by establishing production facilities to manufacture quality fabrics using the natural water resources around Cison. The Veneto area had established links with silk and wool production in neighbouring municipalities, but not until the 1960s did the mass exodus stop as smaller businesses were established.

Feasts

Cison offers year-round entertainment, with musical concerts, plays, puppet shows, art exhibitions and Christmas markets. Specific food and craft events are detailed below.

Assaporando Cison

This food and drink festival takes place over March and April each year, showcasing traditional local products, ancient methods and timeless artisan skills, with live crafts and demonstrations.

Artigianato Vivo

A huge exhibition of craftwork involving master craftsmen from all over Italy. It takes place around the mid-August bank holiday in the streets and districts of Cison di Valmarino. The streets, courtyards and houses open to the world, hosting hundreds of small workshops of skilled artisans who demonstrate particular techniques and individually made products.

Secolare Fiera Franca dei Santi Simone e Giuda

This market, held in Tovena, dates back centuries and is one of the oldest markets around.

Il Presepio

In Mura at Christmas, an outdoor exhibition of around 70 nativity scenes is held, where locals and tourists can wander around the streets enjoying the creativity and ancient craft work.

Places of Interest

Castelbrando

View from Castelbrando

Castelbrando is the most stunning and eye-catching building in the municipality and one that can be seen from most of the surrounding area. I caught a glimpse of it whilst driving and changed my course of direction to find out more about it, eventually driving up a narrow hairpin road only to have to reverse down as I wasn't a hotel guest!

Castelbrando dominates the valley that runs between Vittorio Veneto and Follina. The construction of a hilltop fortification began in the Middle Ages during an early Hungarian invasion. By the 12th century, the Caminesi family had made the fort habitable, building a small villa and a central tower surrounded by a wall.

In the years that followed it became the property of the Venetian Republic before being given, with the surrounding area, as war reparations to Brandolino IV Brandolini, from Forlì, and to Gattamelata, both mercenary leaders at the service of the republic. Subsequently, Gattamelata received a military promotion and relinquished it in full to Brandolini who became its first count.

The Brandolini family transformed the fortress into a magnificent family seat. During the 20th century, the castle was used by the Salesians as a cultural and spiritual centre.

At the end of the 1990s it was sold to Massimo Colomban, who transformed it into a boutique hotel where carefully restored 12th century architecture and 16th century buildings sit side by side with grandiose Baroque flourishes.

To enter the castle is an experience in itself. A panoramic funicular railway takes hotel guests and day visitors up the side of the cliff, where you will find restaurants, bars and a theatre. At an altitude of 400m, it's definitely worth a visit; it's intriguing and beguiling. You can dine, have coffee or visit the museum. The wide terraces surrounded by crenelated walls offer fabulous views of the village of Cison below.

Castelbrando

Sunbathing on the battlements

Restaurant at Castelbrando

Vintage Radio Museum of Cison di Valmarino

For radio fans, this specialised museum is right up your street. The exhibition incorporates equipment from 1920 until the 1970s, highlighting the evolution of technology and the social role played by the radio.

Opening times: Saturday 3-7pm, Sunday 10am-12pm and 3-7pm.

Soller

Nestled in the foothills of the Prealps and surrounded by nature, Soller is the first hamlet along the road to Pieve di Soligo from Vittorio Veneto. This rural location is the start of dozens of different paths and tracks; you can walk in the woods and venture to the San Boldo Pass or to the peak of Mount Cimone, or simply immerse yourself in the beauty of the moraine hill leading to Gai, breathing in an atmosphere of great tranquillity and serenity.

Prealps

I love Castelbrando and would definitely recommend a visit, even if just for coffee. However, for me the picturesque 'pièce de résistance' of this municipality is the stunning village of Rolle, which can be found in the hills south of Cison and is protected by the Italian National Trust (FAI). The famous poet Andrea Zanzotto was very fond of Rolle, calling it "a postcard sent by the gods". It's undisputed land of the famous Prosecco DOCG and without a doubt an awe-inspiring, eye-popping vista on approach around the bend from the south. It's really a perfectly beautiful place where you can enjoy breathtaking views of the manicured rows of vines that stretch as far as the eye can see along the gently undulating slopes.

Rolle

The village of San Boldo, 700 metres above sea level, has been made more prominent because of the structural engineering founded within it, the San Boldo Pass. The Pass is about 10 minutes outside of Tovena along the historic 'Road of 100 Days', characterised by twists and tunnels and a curved axis. More unmissable views unfold at the top to the south: the wall of rocks, the small town of Tovena, the two lakes and the rolling hills of Prosecco vines sloping down to the plains. As with a lot of places in the Prosecco region, it is said on clear days you can see the sea. I haven't yet, but I do enjoy trying.

San Boldo pass

With five tunnels dug into the rock, the road is remembered today for the particularly incredible way it was built in just 100 days using around 7,000 men, hence the name. To commemorate this feat, photographic panels are positioned along its length and located at the top of the pass at the headquarters of the Alpine Tovena, where there is an exhibition dedicated to WWI.

Tovena, another of the striking hamlets found within the municipality, exhibits a certain amount of old-world charm. It has a long history; it appears in the diploma issued by Otto I dated February 2, 962. The name 'Tovena' finds its remote origin in the particular shape of the land on which the small village stands, probably derived from the word 'toff' indicating a harsh and impenetrable terrain. The main square shows only part of the beauty of this area. Alleys and street are full of old stone houses, demonstrating a deeply traditional way of life.

WINERIES

VIGNE MATT S.R.L

Via Tea, 8 località Case Sparse, Rolle, 31030 Cison di Valmarino
(TV)
+39390438975798 | +390438975028
info@vignematte.it | www.vignematte.it

Wine tastings, retail sales, winery visits
Production between 100,000 and 500,000 bottles

Vigne Matt

This winery is set in the most marvellous rural location, less than
10 minutes from Molinetta della Croda, the 17th century
waterwheel. Well signposted, a steep hill lends a certain amount of
grandeur to your arrival. It's difficult to know where to go when you
arrive at the buildings but a slope on the right drops down to the
magnificent tasting area, where the superlative views are among the
finest in the area. Gazing out of the large picture windows is
stunningly spectacular, with lush greenery directly below, leading
to darker green hills and shady grey mountains on the horizon. The
stone-floored room is cavernous, the clear host of many a black-tie
event in this superlative setting. The Prosecco is great too! Award-
winning, of course, and encompasses Dry, Extra Dry and Brut
varieties alongside a smattering of local wines. My visits have been

without an appointment and conducted quite quickly, though I would advise you to book to get a prepared welcome. Check to get an English-speaking guide too; it's not a problem but shouldn't be assumed.

View from the tasting room

Vigne Matt tasting and banqueting room

DUCA DI DOLLE
Via Piai Orientali, n°5 - 31030 Rolle di Cison di Valmarino (Tv)
+390438975809 | +390438975792
info@ducadidolle.it | www.ducadidolle.it

Wine tastings, accommodation, retail sales, vineyard visits
Production up to 150,000 bottles

I've not visited Duca di Dolle but my fellow Prosecco safari group
were staying here for their mini weekend and spoke very highly of
it. Superbly decorated, clean and with huge attention to detail were
attributes I heard. They enjoyed the Prosecco too.

13. FOLLINA

Number of inhabitants: 3,784
Altitude: 191m
Area km²: 24.08
Patron Saint: Pentecost – May 23

Follina is a small, picturesque municipality at the foot of the Belluno Prealps where you will find a stunning piedmont landscape and perfectly preserved historical buildings. At an altitude of around 200 metres above sea level, Follina is located near the end of the Soligo river valley. It's 60km northwest of Venice and 35km north of Treviso and is sited on a significant road junction halfway between Valdobbiadene and Vittorio Veneto.

Hosted by a lush valley rich in woods, sources of water and luxuriant vineyards, Follina lies in a pleasant position and enjoys a mild climate, never too harsh in winter and never too hot in summer.

Follina is a great little town to stay. There are plenty of restaurants, all producing stunning local fare, and it's very centrally located, within easy reach of Conegliano, Veneto Vittoria and Valdobbiadene whilst still being a wonderful town to visit. Alongside the stunning abbey in its significant plot at the head of the road junction, legacy buildings proliferate. It's close to Cison and Castelbrando too, so plenty to occupy you. On my frequent trips to Italy, I try and base myself around Follina; I don't know why, but it calls me back time after time.

History

Artefacts discovered dating from over 120,000 years ago suggest Follina was occupied in pre-historic times. The remains of a path concurrent with the Roman road Via Claudia Augusta has also been identified.

Follina

A big part of Follina's history played out with the founding of the Benedictine Abbey of Santa Maria: a serene piece of 13th-century history with a beautiful inner courtyard, where a profound sense of peace still prevails.

In the 12th century, Cistercian monks settled in Follina; the construction of the abbey was completed in 1268 by monks Arnaldo and Andrea and the master builders Zardino and Armano. The industrious monks began cloth-making activities back then, a legacy that has prevailed and supported the town to the present day, contributing to the name of the municipality.

Abbey of Santa Maria, Follina

The name Follina comes from the word 'follatura', meaning the fulling of wool, a washing and felting technique the monks taught the people of this village in the 11th century.

The Serica della Marca factory is situated just outside the village and supplies silks, yarns and fabrics to the world's most renowned fashion houses.

Walking through the streets around the abbey allows you the opportunity to see the beautiful buildings of the historical centre born during the introduction of industry: Palazzo Barberis Rusca, Palazzo Bernardi, Palazzo Tandura and the former 19th century Andretta woollen mill are notable example of industrial archaeology.

Places of Interest

If you're heading from the south, from Pieve di Soligo, the SP4 passes the Soligo wine shop on the left and the fabulous restaurant Locanda da Lino (well worth a visit) on the right and heads north to Follina, passing several small hamlets on the way.

Soligo wine shop

Locanda da Lino restaurant

The road is a beautiful drive; it's mostly straight, with the odd bend, but the flat drive is so well contrasted against the sight in front of you in the direction you're heading, which has huge lush tree-covered mountains. It's one of my favourite drives.

Road to Follina

Abbey of Santa Maria

This abbey is worth a visit for its idyllic, peaceful beauty. The cloisters are truly serene yet breathtaking and the inside full of surprises, from the twin spiral columns, decoratively adorned and each different to the next, to the Romanesque bell tower and the stone within the cloister wall attesting to its construction in 1268.

Abbey of Santa Maria cloisters

Basilica (Abbey of Santa Maria)

There is a fresco of the angel of the apocalypse that keeps vigil over the monks and the 'capital of bees' at the entrance to the refectory, which reminds the monks that sustenance is the fruit of hard work. The overall effect creates a graceful sense of movement, peace and utmost tranquillity. The wooden baroque crucifix and the 1527 fresco by Francesco da Milano are the most important works of the subsequent centuries. Within the abbey, the 14th century Romano-Gothic church is home to the mysterious image of the Madonna with Child, made in the sandstone of the 6th century, of oriental origin, possibly Nubian, placed in an alcove in the high altar.

The abbey suffered serious damage during the First World War, when it was first used as a cinema for soldiers and then turned into stables. It can be visited every day between 7am-12pm and 2.30-7pm. Entry into the basilica is not allowed during religious functions.

Palazzo Barberis-Rusca

Palazzo Barberis-Rusca is an unimposing 17th century building overlooking the main square of the town, originally connected to the abbey by a wall of low buildings, since demolished. The palazzo was built by Francesco Fadda, who brought significant innovation to the Italian cloth industry back in the 17th century. He took his lead from English and Dutch suppliers, mirroring their production of lighter fabrics and stealing their market share. In 1740, the building became the headquarters of the Tron-Stahl company.

The large wooden central entrance shows clearly the effects of the passage of time: the stone flags have been worn down through years of use and the ground undulates at the bottom of the door. It is an interesting structure that represents the early manufacturing activity which, until the 19th century, characterised the centre of Follina.

Art shop

Head up Via Pallade, keeping the abbey on your right, to find a row of small two-storey buildings and an interesting little artists' gallery. It's hard not to get distracted with the sight of the abbey buildings but stand a moment and view the pale umber building facing you at the top of the street, adjacent to the abbey, which is the Palazzo Bernardi.

Palazzo Bernardi

The abbot Jacopo Bernardi (1813-1897), known for being a writer, professor and famous patriot, resided here. A commemorative stone pays homage to the abbot and bears the date of construction of the building (28th April 1758).

The river flows down Via Roma, which leads from the main square and runs parallel to the Via Martiri della Libertà. Look out for the waterside house with shuttered windows and the featured trowel, just above the waterline.

Palazzo Bernardi

WINERIES

BORGO COL VINI
Via Col, 10, Col, Follina, TV, Italia
+393488976902 | +393488976902
info@alcol.tv | www.borgo.alcol.tv

Wine tastings, accommodation, restaurant, retail sales, sale of
local food products, winery visits, vineyard visits
Production up to 150,000 bottles

This winery is also a working farm, an agriturismo and a restaurant,
very popular with locals for Saturday evening meals. It's out of the
way and very rustic. Our tour included a brief indication of the fields
and the winery before the tasting. Daniele was very informative and
we tasted several different DOCGs plus a local Verdiso wine – a
favourite of mine. Be aware, this is a working farm: the owner deals
with everything and your presentation may be punctuated with
locals collecting supplies.

Borgo Col Prosecco

14. MIANE

Number of inhabitants: 3,252
Altitude: 259m (varies)
Area km²: 30.88
Patron Saint: Natività di Maria Vergine (The Nativity of the Virgin Mary)

Miane is a municipality located about 60km northwest of Venice and about 35km from Treviso, near the border with Belluno in the northern part of the province where the valley ends.

Continuing higher, you will find the peaks of Mount Crep (1346m), Croda Maor, Salvedela (1286m), Monte Corno and Cimone (1438m).

Epic scenery

The municipality is made up of three small and three larger villages that stretch into a hilly green valley called 'la Vallata' at the foot of the Treviso Prealps. It's a largely agricultural area of verdant pastures dotted with small hamlets, cottages scattered here and there and farm buildings synonymous with the most prolific activities of the Mianesi, from which it still derives a great deal of its livelihood: pasture, breeding, wines, chestnuts and dairy products. It's lovely for a rural walk or cycle.

History

Miane probably owes its name to 'Aemilius', a Roman veteran. Its proximity to Ceneda and the via Claudia Augusta Altinate road alludes to its Roman origins. This important Roman-built road connected the Treviso plain with the feudal countries of Northern Italy and Europe with many settlements developing along its length.

The hardships and destruction of two world wars took its toll on the area, leading to mass emigration in search of work. Records from 1956 show the extent of the exodus with almost 1,000 of the 3,735 inhabitants working outside the area, either permanently or temporarily. Economic activity in the 1960s brought an influx of people, stimulating housebuilding and other local activities.

Feasts

Festa dei Marroni a Combai

Combai was the scene of intense partisan activity during WWII, perhaps because of the nature of the landscape and its rural location. Combai is on the slopes of the Madean wood, 395m above sea level, and famous for the traditional chestnut festival. The festival hosts numerous school and interest groups who come from all over the Veneto region to visit the chestnut woods and its harvest. Guided tours are organised in collaboration with the Pro Loco Consortium of the Quartier del Piave.

The Festa dei Marroni takes place around the end of October/early November and offers a full and varied itinerary of activities.

- Culinary feasts include a different dish every day of the week made with chestnuts as a theme.
- Woodland walks through enchanting territory to collect chestnuts and learn about wood ecosystems.
- Arts and crafts exhibitions, music and entertaining activities by woodcarvers, creative painting and weaving workshops, cheese making, polenta preparation and cob cleaning explanations.

The locals are proud of their land and territory and actively promote and enjoy the tradition of their fine produce. Cooking on a spit is a perfect example of their use of traditional methods. Throughout the foothills, the spit is prepared with mixed meats: pork, veal, chicken and rabbit.

Miane district

Local wines such as Verdiso and Perera can be used in small quantities in the production of Prosecco but these wines are not to be ignored in their own right. Verdiso is a legacy grape of the Treviso foothills, used by settlers of the Abbey of Follina as early as 1788. It is straw-yellow in colour and has a subtle, spicy, delicately fruity smell. The flavour is dry, lively, sour, with a hint of unripe apple, medium-bodied, with a slightly bitter aftertaste. Perera, also a legacy wine, is used to increase perfume and aroma. The name is due to the shape of the grape or, according to some, the pear-like taste. Finally, the Bianchetta, mentioned as far back as the 16th century, serves to soften Prosecco in cold years. Along with Verdiso, it is often found in the highest and most problematic areas for farming.

Places of Interest

As with other municipalities, the local churches hold a large display of Italian masters and religious material; however, Miane is deep in the Prosecco area and is largely rural. There are a couple of private Italian villas in this area: Villa Gera Minucci Bellati, rich in furnishings and works of art, and the Villa Bellati, located on the hill overlooking the town of Premaor.

Villa Gera Minucci

Villa Bellati

This is an 18th century villa set among vineyards overlooking the village of Premaor. Built by the Venetian merchant Giacomo Vanello, it was recently purchased by the Gregoletto family, an established wine-making family from Premaor; it was Luigi Gregoletto's ambition to buy the villa where his ancestors worked in service. The central rectangular building has the Vanello family crest and a sundial that shows French, Babylonian and Italian time on three superimposed dials.

WINERIES

GREGOLETTO LUIGI AZIENDA VINICOLA SAS
Via San Martino, 81 - 31050 Premaor Di Miane (TV)
+390438970463
info@gregoletto.com | www.gregoletto.com

Wine tastings, retail sales, winery & vineyard visits
Production listed as between 100,000 and 500,000 bottles

I've visited Gregoletto a couple of times. It's quite easy to find but has a lot of buildings when you get there. It's got a lovely family feel and there's plenty of evidence and stories about the generations. The original building was once a small farmhouse and has been extended, placing an old well, once outside, as a feature inside the updated building; other relics from its past exist within the cool broad walls.

Once outside, now inside the farmhouse

My first visit was a rush in the morning on the way back to the airport – so imagine my surprise when I turned up to find a full Italian breakfast laid out to eat whilst I tasted Prosecco! I was more prepared for my second visit and it still involved food; however, on this occasion the family had placed pairing dishes alongside the respective Prosecco. We had a guided tour of the ancient buildings and then were escorted to their tasting room. Tasting involved a glass of Prosecco matched with their suggested small bites. What a treat!

Tasting with small bites

Gregoletto prosecco

SERRE SPUMANTI Soc. Agr. S.S.
via Casale Vacca, 8 Cambai, Miane (TV)
+390438893502 | +390438899649
info@proseccoserre.com | www.proseccoserre.com

Wine tastings, Retail sales, winery visits
Production listed as between 100,000 and 500,000 bottles

15. VALDOBBIADENE

Number of inhabitants: 10,271
Altitude: 247m
Area km²: 62.90
Patron Saint: St Gregory the Great – second Monday in March

Valdobbiadene is a town in the province of Treviso. Situated in the northeast of Italy, 50km north of Venice and around 100km from the Dolomites, just below the Alpine-Dolomite areas of Veneto, it provides a perfect climate for cultivation of the Glera grape.

Valdobbiadene – main square

Known as the 'city of wine', Valdobbiadene has a proliferation of fields of vines, wineries and retail outlets selling the famous legacy product, Prosecco. One area, San Stefano, is particularly synonymous with Prosecco, with a cascade of vineyards exposed to the sun, interrupted only by ancient farmhouses and old churches. Its vertiginous position shows a privileged view of the Cartizze hill, which is at the heart of the DOCG denomination. These 106 hectares of prime winery real estate are host to some of the finest and most complexly layered Prosecco, planted in the ideal location, with the finest terroir and climatic perfectness to portray freshness, acidity, and the aromas typical of this wine. Fiercely competed for, the land is not owned by a single winery but shared by row, which allows more winemakers to produce their version of the Cartizze.

Valdobbiadene – city of wine

History

Valdobbiadene probably owes its name to its location, alongside the fork split in the Piave river as suggested by the toponym 'Duplavilis'.

As with many municipalities, the lush pastures, water access and amenable climate encouraged early settlement. It is thought the area was inhabited forty thousand years ago with various artefacts proving a continuous human presence from the Mousterian age. The earliest records found date from 1116, when Emperor Henry V arrived in Treviso to resolve the not unusual controversies of the city and rural communities.

Over subsequent centuries, the town was subject to changes of rule as opposing powerful families took charge (the Carraresis, Ezzelino da Romanos, the Da Caminos). Valdobbiadene, continuously traversed by struggles and depredations, fell under Venetian rule around the middle of the 14th century. Feudalism was thus brought to an end.

With the arrival of Napoleon and subsequent Austrian domination, the municipalities arose, first three, then two: Valdobbiadene and San Pietro di Barbozza. At this time the rising bourgeoisie, made up of merchants and landowners, acquired the lands of the Venetian nobility and built imposing buildings around the main square.

Valdobbiadene and the whole Veneto region was returned to Italy from Austria after the First World War, allowing for reconstruction and the development of the viticultural cultivation very much in evidence in the present day.

Places of Interest

San Stefano

If you're visiting Valdobbiadene from the east of the region, I recommend you travel along the high road, the SP36, through the heart of the wine region that's become famous as the finest area for production of Prosecco Superiore.

This road, also a local bus route, travels through the hills from Follina or Miane along a twisty-turny route, demonstrating far-reaching views, panoramic landscapes and lush greenery at every turn, interspersed by tiny hamlets and the inevitable sight of column after column of glorious green vines.

Welcome Prosecco lovers to Osteria Senz 'Oste

Osteria Senz 'Oste translates as 'the bar without a host' and can be found along the SP36 in San Stefano in the direction of Valdobbiadene. Located down a dirt track just past the Ca Salina winery on the left, the Osteria Senz Oste is a small unpoliced watering hole for those wishing to enjoy the sunny vista and to buy a bottle of local, unbranded Prosecco on the hillside from a vending machine. Take euros, as British credit cards don't seem to work. For 10-15 euros you can obtain a bottle of Cartizze Prosecco and while away the hours on top of a hillside in the glorious sunshine. (A warning: the path up is hewn out of the hillside and quite steep.)

The old farm building has remained the same since the 1950s and, despite its newer neighbour, still maintains its original façade, both inside and out. The kitchen is decorated with notes from fellow travellers and has a working fridge where cheeses and meats can be purchased via the honesty box.

I love its atmosphere, its tranquillity and the 'top of the world' feeling. It's become more popular of late and has developed in size with a growing local patronage, which has unfortunately destroyed some of its quaintness.

Parking can be a problem and the nearby winery is always busy – don't be tempted to park in their small car park. The drive down the rough track is also quite tricky; parking on the main road is a better option, and there's a layby opposite the rough track.

Prosecco bottle vending machine

Seats with a view – Osteria Senz'Oste

And what a view!

The Modigliani of the Piave is a combination of funny figures, strange characters, animals and floral arrangements, made using the smooth stones of the Piave, whose oval and oblong shapes make the faces reminiscent of those portrayed by Amedeo Modigliani. They can be seen by the side of the road in San Pietro di Barbozza: turn left off the SP36 onto Via della Cima. For the unsuspecting, it's a refreshing, quirky surprise. The creator of these works is Antonio Zoe Favaro, who spent his working life as a bricklayer. On retiring, he started to create these original sculptures. His works are not for sale but can be obtained by making a donation to local causes such as the local kindergarten.

Modigliani del Piave

Villa dei Cedri

This villa can be found on Via Piva, on the road into Valdobbiadene. The villa was built in the 1800s by Pietro Piva, a silk expert, who demolished a large part of the old village of Martignago around the factory to make room for the villa. It was designed according to the tastes of the period and has its own park, a private enclosure with high fences surrounding the villa. Alongside the villa, Pietro Piva re-purposed the 18th century wheat mill to use for his silk spinning business. Piva traded in exceptional quality silk and had machinery to accommodate the manufacture of this. The business eventually outgrew the premises and was relocated whilst the original building still stands.

Villa Cedri

Its current appearance dates back to the early 20th century and it is now in public ownership. Each August, it hosts the event Goblets of Stars and for many years it was the site of the National Exhibition of Sparkling Wines, the oldest and most important wine industry review. In recent years, its halls have also hosted the Artistic

Nativity Scene of Valdobbiadene. The building is surrounded by a vast park open to the public, in which there is a play area for children.

Santa Maria Assunta

The cathedral is situated in the main square, Piazza Marconi, and was originally built with three naves, but underwent radical restoration sometime between the 15th and 18th centuries, which gave it its current neoclassical style. The building was destroyed by bombing during the First World War and was later rebuilt. It contains works by artists such as Francesco da Conegliano, Paris Bordon and also Palma il Giovane.

Santa Maria Assunta

The bell tower, built between 1743-1767 and designed by the architect Francesco Maria Preti of Castelfranco, is separated from the cathedral by a busy road. It too suffered severe damage during the First World War and was restored in the following years. Today, it is considered the symbol of Valdobbiadene. The sundial, with its solar zodiac calendar, built in the first half of the 19th century, was also destroyed by the bombing. Thankfully it is now fully restored and once more visible on the south side of the tower.

Slightly off the main square (take the road by the side of the wine shop) you will see the war memorial, located at the end of Viale della Vittoria. It was designed by Treviso sculptor Toni Benneton in honour of the fallen of two world wars. In the central part of the monument, raised by a series of steps, wrought iron figures represent the story of Christ.

Valdobbiadene – war memorial

<u>San Floriano</u>

The first record of the sanctuary dedicated to San Floriano, located in prime position overlooking the town centre, is in a will dated 1424. Over the centuries it has been rebuilt and enlarged several times, with the lighthouse bell tower added in 1802. This small oratory suffered severe damage during the bombing of 1917-18 and was later rebuilt, with the addition of the square in front of the church, almost a viewpoint from which you can drink in the stunning views over the Valdobbiadene area.

San Floriano

View over Valdobbiadene from San Floriano

View from San Stefano

WINERIES

AGOSTINETTO BRUNO Az. Agr.

Strada Piander, 7, Saccol, Valdobbiadene, TV, Italia
+390423972884
info@agostinetto.com | www.agostinetto.com

Wine tastings, retail sales, winery & vineyard visits
Production up to 150,000 bottles

AZ. AGR. AL CANEVON

Al Canevon silver medal winner
Via Pra Fontana, 99, Valdobbiadene, TV, Italia
+390423972403 | +390423905139
info@alcanevon.it | www.alcanevon.com

Silver medal winning wine

Wine tastings, retail sales, winery & vineyard visits Production up to 150,000 bottles

I've visited this winery. It's not much to look at from the outside, and situated in a rather industrial area, but the welcome is great. They fall over themselves to help you and their products are just really lovely to taste, light and sparkling. The Brut Nature is something I buy regularly.

Definitely worth a try!

BELLUSSI SPUMANTI srl
Via Erizzo, 215, Valdobbiadene, TV, Italia
+390423983411 | +390423983477
info@bellussi.com | www.bellussi.com

Wine tastings, retail sales, winery visits

BISOL 1542
Via Follo, 33, Santo Stefano, TV, Italia
+390423900138
info@bisol.it | www.bisol.it

Wine tastings, retail sales, winery visits
Production of over 1,000,000 bottles

BORTOLIN F.lli
Via Menegazzi, 5, Santo Stefano, TV, Italia
+390423900135 | +390423901042
info@bortolin.com | www.bortolin.com

Wine tastings, retail sales, winery visits
Production is between 100,000 and 500,000 bottles

BORTOLIN ANGELO SPUMANTI
Strada di Guia, 107, Valdobbiadene, TV, Italia
+39 0423 900125 | +39 0423 901015
info@bortolinangelo.com | www.bortolinangelo.com

Wine tastings, retail sales, winery & vineyard visits
Production between 100,000 and 500,000 bottles

This winery is a good example of classic Italian styling; the tasting
room is designed with that in mind. It is situated on the road to
Guia and very easy to find. As a slightly bigger winery, they work
hard at developing their products. I've been lucky enough to taste

their Prosecco, both in Italy and in the UK. They are friendly and proactive and will follow up after visits to make sure you enjoyed it.

Bortolin winery

Outside Bortolin Angelo

BORTOLOMIOL S.P.A.
Via Garibaldi Giuseppe, 142, Valdobbiadene, TV, Italia
+3904239749 | +390423975066
info@bortolomiol.com | www.bortolomiol.com

Wine tastings, retail sales, winery & vineyard visits
Production over 1,000,000 bottles

BORTOLOTTI
Via Ruio D'Arcane, 6, Valdobbiadene, TV, Italia
+390423975668
info@bortolotti.com | www.bortolotti.com

Wine tastings, retail sales, winery visits
Production between 500,000 and 1,000,000 bottles

CA' DAL MOLIN
Via Cornoler, 22, San Giovanni, Valdobbiadene, TV, Italia
+390423981017
cadalmolin1@gmail.com

Wine tastings, retail sales, winery & vineyard visits
Production up to 150,000 bottles

Az. Agr. Cà dei ZAGO
via Roccolo, 6 Valdobbiadene
+390423975395
info@cadeizago.it

Wine tastings, accommodation, retail sales, winery & vineyard visits
Production up to 150,000 bottles

CANELLO DOMENICO

via Cesen, 5 Valdobbiadene
+393475735966 | +390423972760
info@ninocanello.it | www.ninocanello.it

Wine tastings, retail sales, winery visits
Production up to 150,000 bottles

CA 'SALINA

Via Santo Stefano, 2, Santo Stefano, Valdobbiadene, TV, Italia
+390423975296
info@casalinaprosecco.it | www.casalinaprosecco.it

Wine tastings, retail sales, winery & vineyard visits
Production between 100,000 and 500,000 bottles

Ca' Salina Prosecco

This winery offers stunning views and a seamless tasting service. I would always recommend booking a wine tasting as one-to-one service will be guaranteed. However, if you have a little time left over, Gregorio is your man and will offer you a taste of his range of superb Prosecco. He's fluent in both English and German, along with his native Italian, of course.

This was the very first winery I visited, recommended by my hotel, and it's a beautiful example of a great drive into the hills and a fabulous range of Prosecco.

Ca' Salina winery

When you arrive, look around at the scenery and breathe in the view; it's difficult not to be completely bowled over by it. Gregorio is a workaholic, always ready to engage in, inform and entertain his guests. He does talk fast, so be prepared to tune in.

Ca' Salina Prosecco is beautiful, light and fresh; it's the first bottle I bought and the one I return to frequently. I use several in my food pairing dinners.

View from the Ca' Salina winery

Az. Agr. CAMPION di GATTO G.& f. ss

Via Campion, 2, Valdobbiadene, TV, Italia
+390423980432
info@campionspumanti.it | www.campionspumanti.it

Wine tastings, accommodation, retail sales and winery visits
Production up to 150,000 bottles

Campion is an agriturismo, a working farm, complete with a Border
Collie with a sense of fun. Rustic and charming with a bustling feel
to it, you'll need the satnav to find it as it's deep in the countryside
and down a long, bumpy entrance track unsuitable for coaches. The

accommodation is set out around a pool. I'd love to stay and enjoy the calm, rural atmosphere but haven't managed to book it yet.

Above: Entrance to Campion Agriturismo. Below: Campion Prosecco

CANEVEL SPUMANTI
Via Rocat e Ferrari 17, Valdobbiadene
+390423975940
segreteria@canevel.it | www.canevel.it

Wine tastings, retail sales, winery & vineyard visits
Production between 500,000 and 1,000,000 bottles

I haven't been to the winery but have tasted Canevel in the wine
shop on Valdobbiadene main square; it stocks a variety of products.

CANTINA PONTE VECCHIO
via Val de Faveri, 1 Valdobbiadene
+390423981363 | +390423981363
floriano@pontevecchio.tv.it | www.pontevecchio.tv.it

Wine tasting, retail sales and winery visits
No further information given

CANTINE VEDOVA di Vedova Luigi & C. snc
Via Erizzo, 6, Valdobbiadene, TV, Italia
+390423972037 | +390423972404
cantine@cantinevedova.com | www.cantinevedova.com

Wine tasting, accommodation, restaurant, retail sales, winery
visits
Production over 1,000,000 bottles

CIODET SPUMANTI
Via Piva, 104, Valdobbiadene, TV, Italia
+390423973131
prosecco@ciodet.it | www.ciodet.it

Wine tastings, retail sales & winery visits
Production between 100,000 and 500,000 bottles

COLESEL Spumanti srl
Via Vettorazzi e Bisol, 2, Santo Stefano, TV, Italia
+390423901055
info@colesel.it | www.colesel.it

Wine tastings, retail sales & winery visits
Production between 100,000 and 500,000 bottles

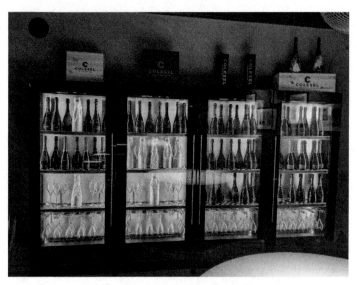

Well stocked fridges at Colesel

I immediately warmed to Laura, my host at Colesel. She was super friendly and informative whilst giving me tasting glasses of some fabulous Prosecco. The bottles are wrapped in paper showing the geography of the winery. Unusually, they produce three different Cartizze Proseccos: an Extra Brut, a Brut and a Dry. All complex tasting and all fabulous, of course. They also offer a Prosecco picnic, which would be lovely on a sunny day and well worth a try!

Tasting experience at Colesel

COL VETORAZ Spumanti srl
Str. delle Treziese, 1, 31049 Valdobbiadene, TV, Italia
T +390423975291 | F +390423975571
info@colvetoraz.it | www.colvetoraz.it

Wine tasting and retail sales
Production over 1,000,000 bottles

Driving through the region, you will never become used to the panoramic views, the endless photo opportunities and the lush, vine-covered hills that seem to proliferate around every bend in the road. This company plays host to the million-dollar view, overlooking the Cartizze hill and through the valley as far as the eye can see. It's a bustling, busy tasting room, with plenty of variety in fabulous Prosecco, but I would suggest booking if you want to sample their luscious production.

Above: Col Vetoraz Winery. Below: Col Vetoraz Prosecco

SOC.AGR.DALLA LIBERA SS

via Val, 20 Valdobbiadene (TV)
+393206266944
ss.dallalibera@gmail.com

Wine tasting, retail sales
Production up to 150,000 bottles

DEA SOCIETA' AGRICOLA di Caldart A. & C. ss

Vicolo Longher, 3, Bigolino, TV, Italia
+390423971017 | +390423905031
info@dearivalta.it | www.dearivalta.it

Wine tastings, retail sales, sale of local food products
Production listed as up to 150,000 bottles

DOMUS-PICTA

Via Arcol, 51, Valdobbiadene, TV, Italia
+390423973971 | +390423978970
commerciale@domus-picta.com | www.domus-picta.com

Wine tastings, accommodation, retail sales, winery & vineyard
visits
Production between 500,000 and 1,000,000 bottles

AZ. AGR DRUSIAN FRANCESCO

via Anche, 1, Bigolino, Valdobbiadene (TV)
+390423982151 | +390423980000
drusian@drusian.it | www.drusian.it

Wine tastings, retail sales, winery & vineyard visits
Production over 1,000,000 bottles

FASOL MENIN SOC. AGR.
Via Fasol e Menin, 22/b, Valdobbiadene, TV, Italia
+390423974262 | +390423905603
myprosecco@fasolmenin.com | www.fasolmenin.com

Wine tasting, retail sales and winery visits
Production up to 150,000 bottles

FOSS MARAI
Strada di Guia, 109, Valdobbiadene, TV, Italia
+390423900570
info@fossmarai.com | www.fossmarai.com

Wine tasting, retail sales
Production of between 500,000 and 1,000,000

Az. Agr, FRATELLI COLLAVO s.s.
Via Fossetta, 4 - 31049 Valdobbiadene
+393335824047
info@fratellicollavo.com | www.fratellicollavo.com

Wine tasting, retail sales, winery & vineyard visits
Production up to 150,000 bottles

FRATELLI GATTO CAVALIER
via Cartizze, 1 Valdobbiadene
+390423985338
info@fratelligattocavalier.it | www.fratelligattocavalier.it

Wine tasting, retail sales, sales of local products, winery &
vineyard visits
Production up to 150,000 bottles

Rural Valdobbiadene

FROZZA s.s. Az. Agr.
via Martiri 31, Colbertaldo, Vidor (TV)
+390423987069 | +390423987069
valdobbiadene@frozza.it

Retail sales, winery visits
Production up to 150,000 bottles

GARBARA
Via Menegazzi, 119, Santo Stefano, TV, Italia
+390423900155
info@garbara.it | www.garbara.it

Restaurant & retail sales
Production up to 150,000 bottles

GEMIN SPUMANTI - Bortolomiol Guglielmo srl
Via Erizzo, 187, Valdobbiadene, TV, Italia
+390423975450 | +390423976146
info@spumantigemin.it | www.spumantigemin.it

Wine tasting, retail sales & winery visits
Production up to 150,000 bottles

GUIA
Strada Fontanazze, 2/a, Guia, TV, Italia
+390423900421 | +390423901108
info@aziendaagricolaguia.it | www.aziendaagricolaguia.com

Wine tasting, restaurant, retail sales, winery & vineyard visits
Production up to 150,000 bottles

RIVA DEI FRATI
via Callonga, 5, Follo, Valdobbiadene
+390423639798 | +390423639811
info@rivadeifrati.it | www.rivadeifrati.it

Open to the public but no further details
Production up to 150,000 bottles

IL FOLLO
Via Follo, 36, Santo Stefano, TV, Italia
+390423901092 | +390423900000
agriturismo@ilfollo.it | www.ilfollo.it

Accommodation, retail sales, sale of local food products
Production of between 100,000 to 500,000 bottles

LA CASA VECCHIA
Via Callonga, 8, Santo Stefano, TV, Italia
+390423900160
info@lacasavecchia.it | www.lacasavecchia.it

Wine tastings, accommodation, retail sales, sale of local food
products, winery & vineyard visits
Production up to 150,000 bottles

La Casa Vecchia Prosecco

With so many wineries to choose from, it's difficult to differentiate
and I do like to see something a little inventive or different from the
norm. La Casa Vecchia do something I've seen in France but not in
the Prosecco region before; they advertise the option to adopt a row
of vines and you can receive your own labelled bottle of Prosecco.
They also offer tastings on Saturday afternoons, complete with
Alpine cheeses and local sweets. We visited during the week, were
hosted by Emanuele and shown around the premises, including the
accommodation; one room has a fantastic balcony overlooking the
vines. The tasting area was cool and rustic. They produce around

30,000 bottles. The Prosecco Superiore was fabulous. It was difficult to choose just one to bring home and I will definitely be adopting my own row of vines in the future.

On a subsequent visit, I stayed in the accommodation at La Casa Vecchia and was lucky enough to be given the room with the balcony overlooking the vineyard. It's a very central location for wineries with several within walking distance.

Balcony at La Casa Vecchia

Stunning view from La Casa Vecchia accommodation

LE BERTOLE DI BORTOLIN G. & C. Soc. Agr. S.S.

Via Europa, 20, Valdobbiadene, TV, Italia
+390423975332 | +390423905007
info@lebertole.it | www.lebertole.it

Wine tasting, retail sales & winery visits
Production is listed as between 100,000 and 500,000 bottles

AZ. AGR. LE COLTURE

Via Follo, 5, Santo Stefano, TV, Italia
+390423900192 | +390423900511
info@lecolture.it | www.lecolture.com

Wine tasting, accommodation, retail sales winery & vineyard visits
Production is listed as between 500,000 and 1,000,000 bottles

Tasting glasses at Le Colture

I came across this winery purely by accident after I got slightly lost
and turned up at Le Colture unannounced! They were gracious

enough to invite me in for a tasting. The winery is deep in the heart of San Stefano and within walking distance of a couple of agriturismo (accommodation), so could easily be visited on foot. They have a full and varied selection of wines including Prosecco, Prosecco rosé and red.

LE MASIERE Az. Agr. di Miotto Giampaolo

Strada nuova delel Grave, 7, Santo Stefano di Valdobbiadene, TV, Italia
+393396399183
giampaolo.miotto@alice.it | lemasiere.com

Wine tasting, retail sales, winery & vineyard visits
Production listed as up to 150,000 bottles

MARSURA NATALE Soc. Agr. s.s.

Strada Fontanazze, 4, Guia, TV, Italia
+390423901054 | +390423904719
info@marsuraspumanti.it | www.marsuraspumanti.it

Open to the public, no further information supplied

MARSURET

Via Barch, 17, Guia, TV, Italia
+390423900139
marsuret@marsuret.it | www.marsuret.it

Wine tasting, retail sales & winery visits
Production listed as between 100,000 and 500,000 bottles

MIONETTO

via Colderove, 2 Valdobbiadene
+3904239707
mionetto@mionetto.it | www.mionetto.com

Wine tasting, retail sales and winery visits
Production of over 1,000,000 bottles

Glera grape harvest

NANI RIZZI
Via Stanghe, 22, Guia, TV, Italia
+390423900645 | +390423900042
info@nanirizzi.it | www.nanirizzi.it

Wine tasting, retail sales winery & vineyard visits
Production listed as between 500,000 and 1,000,000 bottles

NINO FRANCO SPUMANTI srl

Via Giuseppe Garibaldi, 147, Valdobbiadene, TV, Italia
+390423972051 | +390423975977
info@ninofranco.it | www.ninofranco.it

Wine tasting, accommodation, retail sales & winery visits
Production listed as between 500,000 and 1,000,000 bottles

Soc. Agr. PEDERIVA di Pederiva Walter e Mariangela

Via Cal del Grot, 1/1, Guia, TV, Italia
+390423900143
info@spumantipederiva.com | spumantipederiva.com

Wine tasting, accommodation, retail sales & winery visits
Production listed as between 100,000 and 500,000 bottles

Az Agr REBULI ANGELO & FIGLI S.A.

Strada di Saccol, 40 Saccol di Valdobbiadene
+390423973307 | +390423974214
info@rebuli.it | www.rebuli.it

Wine tasting, accommodation, retail sales & winery visits
Production listed as between 500,000 and 1,000,000 bottles

Az Agr TENUTA RIVALUCE DI ALESSANDRO FAVERO

Strada di Barbozza 1, San Pietro di Barbozza, Valdobbiadene, TV, Italia
+393403211749
info@rivaluce.it | www.rivaluce.it

Wine tasting, retail sales, winery & vineyard visits
Production listed as up to 150,000 bottles

Az Agr ROCCAT
Via Roccat e Ferrari, 1, Valdobbiadene, TV, Italia
+390423972839 | +390423971772
info@roccat.com | www.roccat.com

Wine tasting, accommodation, retail sales, winery & vineyard
visits
Production listed as up to 150,000 bottles

RUGE
Via Foss 1, Valdobbiadene, TV, Italia
+390423900224
info@ruge.it | www.ruge.it

Wine tastings, retail sales, winery visits, vineyard visits
Production listed as up to 150,000 bottles

RUGGERI
Via Pra Fontana, 4, Valdobbiadene, TV, Italia
+3904239092
ruggeri@ruggeri.it | www.ruggeri.it

Wine tasting, retail sales, winery & vineyard visits
Production of over 1,000,000 bottles

SAN GREGORIO
Via San Gregorio, 18, Valdobbiadene, TV, Italia
+390423975534
info@proseccosangregorio.it | www.proseccosangregorio.it

Wine tasting, retail sales, winery & vineyard visits
Production up to 150,000 bottles

This boutique winery is most definitely one of my top three! Their
wines are superb, and well sought after at my tasting events. San

Gregorio is a winery I've visited many times and I am on good terms with Elisa, who is front of house. They only produce DOCG Prosecco and it really is superb, award-winning and delicious!

San Gregorio DOCG prosecco production

I particularly enjoy their fresh and effervescent frizzante, and the tranquillo, which I feel is a very elegant drink. I use them both at my tasting events. However, I could also rave about the Brut Millesimato. If you book a tasting with them, you'll see what I mean. For me, it really demonstrates the difference between DOCG and DOC quality. The winery is a real family affair: Mum Paola assists, where appropriate; she doesn't speak English but tries her best to communicate and her humour and personality shine through. She's generally accompanied by Rocky the dog, a mischievous Labrador.

San Gregorio tranquillo, frizzante and spumante

SANTA EUROSIA
Via della Cima, 8, 31049 Valdobbiadene, TV, Italia
+390423973236
info@santaeurosia.it | www.santaeurosia.it

Wine tasting, retail sales and winery visits
Production between 100,000 and 500,000 bottles

SANTANTONI
Via Cimitero, 52, Santo Stefano, Valdobbiadene, TV, Italia
+390423900226
info@santantoni.it | www.santantoni.it

Wine tasting, retail sales, sale of local food products, winery &
vineyard visits
Production up to 150,000 bottles

SILVANO FOLLADOR Az. Agr

via Callonga 11, Località Follo, Santo Stefano di Valdobbiadene
+390423900295
info@silvanofollador.it | www.silvanofollador.it

Wine tasting and retail sales
Production up to 150,000 bottles

SOMASOT di SANZOVO PAOLO Società Semplice Agr

via San Giacomo 2, fraz. Bigolino, 31049 Valdobbiadene
+390423980523
info@sanzovo.it | www.sansovo.it

Wine tasting, retail sales, sales of local produce, winery & vineyard visits
Production up to 150,000 bottles

SUI NUI SPUMANTI

via Cal Fontana 15B, 31049 Valdobbiadene
+3904231916793
info@suinuispumanti.it | www.suinuispumanti.it

E-Commerce, retail sales & vineyard visits
No further information given

TANORE

Str. Mont, 4A, 31049 Valdobbiadene TV, Italia
+390423975770
info@tanore.it | www.tanore.it

Wine tastings, retail sales winery & vineyard visits
Production up to 150,000 bottles

TERRE DI SAN VENANZIO

Via Capitello Ferrari, 1, Valdobbiadene, TV, Italia
+390423974083 | +390423974093
info@terredisanvenanzio.it | www.terredisanvenanzio.it

Wine tastings, retail sales and winery visits
Production of between 100,000 and 500,000 bottles

What a lovely surprise! I've been to the Prosecco area many times over the last six or seven years but it's always wonderful to find another gem, and no matter how many times I travel here, there are always more people to meet, more superb wines to taste and more things to learn and discover.

Terre di San Venanzio

San Venanzio is the patron saint of Valdobbiadene, the heart of the Prosecco region, and this winery takes its name from this aged legacy. A family-owned business, I was met by Monica, who regaled me with tales of the history of San Venanzio but also the story of their award-winning Prosecco. They had just returned from

Vinitaly, the international exposition, having gained a rare achievement with 96 points and best sparkling (Migliore Spumante) in the 5StarWines competition for their Cartizze. The competition is a blind tasting, on the basis of a careful visual and olfactory analysis, judged over a three-day period. Wines achieving over 90 points are subject to a further analysis by the Scientific Committee and inclusion in the 5Star Wines book.

As you can imagine, the Cartizze is very popular, but limited due to its background. On my second visit, I emailed Monica to ask if we could taste the Cartizze. She saved the very last bottle of the year's production for my visit – how wonderful!

Majoring on quality, they work with the oenologist to prepare award-winning Prosecco and produce Conegliano-Valdobbiadene Prosecco alongside one from the Asolo area, so the visitor can get a real appreciation for the difference in taste and terroir between the two consortiums. I would also recommend their Prosecco Superiore Brut Demi-Long – it's superb! A visit here is a real must.

Prosecco from Terre di San Venanzio

TENUTA GUARDIAN
Via Mas e Chiodari, 5 Fraz. San Giovanni, 31049 Valdobbiadene, TV, Italia
+393493086898
tenutaguardian@hotmail.com

Wine tastings, retail sales, winery & vineyard visits
Production up to 150,000 bottles

TENUTA TORRE ZECCHEI di Eli Spagnol & C. ss soc Agr
Via Capitello Ferrari, 3/a, Valdobbiadene, TV, Italia
+390423976183 | +390423905041
info@torrezecchei.it | www.torrezecchei.it

Wine tastings, retail sales and winery visits
Production of between 100,000 and 500,000 bottles

VAL DE CUNE
Via Spinade, 41, Guia, TV, Italia
+390423901112
info@valdecune.it | www.valdecune.it

Wine tastings, retail sales, winery visits
Production up to 150,000 bottles

VAL D'OCA SRL
Via San Giovanni, 45, San Giovanni, Valdobbiadene, TV, Italia
+390423982070 | +390423982097
valdoca@valdoca.com | www.valdoca.com

Wine tastings, retail sales and winery visits
Production of over 1,000,000 bottles

VALDO SPUMANTI srl
Via Foro Boario, 20, Valdobbiadene, TV, Italia
+3904239090 | +390423972546
info@valdo.com | www.valdo.com

Wine tastings, retail sales, winery & vineyard visits
Production of over 1,000,000 bottles

VALDOC SARTORI Soc Agr ss
Via Menegazzi, 7, Santo Stefano, TV, Italia
+390423900278 | +390423900278
info@valdocsartori.it | www.valdocsartori.it

Wine tastings, retail sales and winery visits
No further information given

VARASCHIN MATTEO e figli snc
Strada Chiesa, 10, Valdobbiadene, TV, Italia
+390423973553 | +390423971758
info@varaschin.com | www.varaschin.com

Wine tastings, winery visits
Production between 100,000 and 500,000 bottles

VIGNE SAVIE
Via Follo, 26, Santo Stefano, TV, Italia
+390423900235 | +391782240818
info@vignesavie.it | www.vignesavie.it

Wine tastings, retail sales & winery visits
Production up to 150,000 bottles

Az. Agr. VIGNETO VECIO

Via Grave, 8, Santo Stefano, Valdobbiadene, TV, Italia
+390423900338 | +39423904768
info@vignetovecio.it | www.vignetovecio.it

Wine tastings, accommodation, restaurant, retail sales, winery &
vineyard visits
Production up to 150,000 bottles

I love this little place; it's so friendly and welcoming. I visited twice
on my last trip to the area, first on my own on the day I arrived, and
then again taking guests two days later, as I enjoyed the experience
so much!

Vigneto Vecio Prosecco

It's an agriturismo with six bedrooms and a restaurant serving local, home-grown food. It's a very central location for those wishing to stay overnight in Valdobbiadene with other wineries very close by; however, you might have to drag yourself away from the fine Prosecco they produce!

I tried a Rive di Santa Stefano, level 5 on the Prosecco pyramid of quality, which they produce a small quantity of, numbering the bottles. I also tried a Col Fondo Prosecco. I thought both were superb and purchased them.

Apparently, during the summer months they serve the Col Fondo in demijohns, which they deliver to your home – if only!

Views along the Prosecco road

ZUCCHETTO Paolo Az. Agr.
Via della Cima, 16, 31049 Valdobbiadene TV, Italia
+393406015848 | +390423971744
sales@zucchetto.com | www.zucchetto.com

Wine tastings, retail sales, winery visits
Production up to 150,000 bottles

I ordered some wine to try, and did a tasting using it. The one I chose from their production was one with a second fermentation in the bottle (Sui Lieveti) as a very different example of Prosecco. Interestingly, all the guys really liked it; it was slightly cloudy in comparison to the usual crystal-clear Prosecco – to be expected, of course, because of the yeast in the bottle. A very drinkable Prosecco!

16. VIDOR

Number of inhabitants: 3,694
Altitude: 152m
Area km²: 13.43
Patron Saint: San Giuseppe – March 19

Vidor, next door to Valdobbiadene, is another important wine-making location. With a picturesque natural landscape, it is particularly distinguished for the production of Prosecco among the vineyards of the Colbertaldo hills.

A drive northward from the Piave River takes you to the Prosecco DOCG area, characterised by cultivated hills where the manual work done by the wine-makers is very much in evidence. On the slopes facing north there are wooded patches with native tree such as hornbeam, ash, chestnut, oak, maple, juniper, hazel and hawthorn. To crown this natural heritage, there are many sites of historical and cultural importance.

Tasting opportunity?

History

Vidor was part of the route of the Via Claudia Augusta, probably because of its proximity to the river. The discovery of a necropolis points to the area being the site of a Roman garrison.

In the Middle Ages, a river port regulated access to the bridge. A Benedictine abbey was built, taking control of the river crossing. The cloister is decorated with columns reminiscent of those of Follina, as well as frescoes from various periods, including a 13th century one of San Cristoforo, the patron saint of travellers and ferrymen. Unfortunately, access to the abbey is not permitted; however, it is possible to walk around the perimeter.

A new stone bridge built to replace the wooden one was completed in 1871 but was destroyed to cover the retreat after the Italian defeat at Caporetto. Vidor was the setting for one of the bloodiest battles of the conflict, on 10 November 1917, when Prussian troops disguised as Italian soldiers launched a ferocious attack on the Italian army, killing more than 300 men and setting the town on fire.

Feasts

Palio di Vidor is celebrated during the second week of September. This is an opportunity for much local rivalry to be seen as teams of four individuals 'storm' the castle by running up the very steep hill to it. The timed and scored event is followed by celebrations. The competition is inspired by a 10th century Hungarian assault against Vidor Castle.

Places of Interest

The origins of the Sanctuary of the Madonna delle Grazie correspond with the arrival of the servants of Mary of the convent of Santa Caterina di Treviso, between 1346 and 1353, following the spread of the bubonic plague. It fell into disuse during the 18th century decline and was re-purposed in the 19th century as a cholera hospital. In recent times, the sanctuary has been restored and is now a destination for pilgrimages. The adjoining convent has been partially restored and now hosts various events, in particular the Celebrations of the Madonna delle Grazie (first two weekends of July), the Pan & Vin (5 January), and the Prosecco Wine Show (April-May).

Rows of vines in Vidor

WINERIES

ADAMI
Via Rovede, 27 - 31020 Colbertaldo di Vidor
+390423982110, +393205638058
info@adamispumanti.it, welcome@adamispumanti.it |
www.adamispumanti.it

Wine tastings, retail sales, winery & vineyard visits
Production between 100,000 and 500,000 bottles

Adami Rive and Cartizze

This winery is a good choice for a real variety of different Prosecco,
including 2 Rive Prosecco and a Cartizze. Not all producers have a

Cartizze in their range and as it's the finest Prosecco made, it's nice to have the opportunity to try it. I love this place and have visited many times; it's definitely in my top five. The entrance area is obvious and elegant, leading to a light, modern tasting room. Adami has two different Rive Prosecco, both complex and full bodied, different from what you're expecting and so different from each other it's difficult to decide on a favourite.

Producing a Rive from a single vineyard in a single year can be a risky business. One bad day of hail can wipe out a whole year's production, which is what has happened quite recently. They also produce a Prosecco made using Glera but adding Chardonnay grapes (within specified limits, of course). It's a refreshing change and is evidence of my absolute belief that not all Proseccos are the same. I use one of their Rive, the Col Credas, on my Prosecco tasting dinners, paired with pork in mustard sauce. It complements the food beautifully!

Ready for tasting at Adami

I've taken the vineyard walk many times. It's a 5-minute car ride away, up the expected slope, but is short, so not too arduous. There's a wonderful perfumed walk past pomegranate and fig trees with spectacular views over the southern edge of the region. Your host will explain about the weeping vines, the age of the trees and the legacy of the vineyard. It's a lovely experience and not too taxing, although not suitable for anyone with walking difficulties. Back at the tasting room, it is possible to arrange a tasting with light bites of local hams and cheeses. Different glasses are set out for each Prosecco. It's a real experience and I'm sure will make you reach for your wallet to purchase the truly different offerings.

BACIO DELLA LUNA SPUMANTI S.r.l.
Via Rovede, 36, 31020 Vidor, TV, Italia
+390423983111 | +390423983100
info@baciodellaluna.it | www.baciodellaluna.it

Not open to the public
Production over 1,000,000 bottles

SOC. AGR. CASTELLO SS di BERTON ITALO e figli
Via Roma 178 Vidor
+393473121060
agr.castello@libero.it | www.castellodibertonvini.it

Wine tastings, retail sales, winery & vineyard visits
Production up to 150,000 bottles

COL DEL LUPO
Via Rovede, 37 - Colbertaldo di Vidor (TV)
+390423980249
info@coldellupo.it | www.coldellupo.it

Production up to 150,000 bottles

An intimate family winery, the tasting room adjoins the family house but doesn't lack facilities and gives it a homely feel. The atmosphere created by Giulia is a very pleasant, professional one, steeped in a deep passion for their wines. They are progressing towards a fully organic winery, a process that takes three years; part of the process involves reducing the sulphates used. They produce 40,000 bottles including a Col Fondo, which is made through the classic method, with the second fermentation carried out in the bottle. Worth a visit.

Col del Lupo tasting

SPUMANTI DAL DIN s.r.l.
via Montegrappa. 29 Vidor (TV)
+390423987295 | +390423989070
daldin@daldin.it | www.daldin.it

Wine tastings, retail sales, winery visits
Production between 100,000 and 500,000 bottles

DE FAVERI SPUMANTI
Via Sartori, 21, 31020 Vidor TV
+390423987673
info@defaverispumanti.it | www.defaverispumanti.it

Wine tastings, retail sales, winery & vineyard visits
Production between 500,000 AND 1,000,000 bottles

I visited this family winery on a sunny afternoon. Giorgia showed me around the bottling plant and the processing area. She was a font of useful information; she and her brother share responsibility for the business. The tasting room, on the first floor, is a large area where I was able to taste several fabulous bottles. They have a Superiore di Cartizze – a Dry Prosecco with 24g of residual sugar, which was a real treat. My personal favourite was the superbly elegant Brut. Definitely one to savour.

De Faveri Prosecco

FROZZA s.s. Az. Agr.
via Martiri 31, Colbertaldo, Vidor (TV)
+390423987069 | +390423987069
valdobbiadene@frozza.it

Wine tastings, retail sales and winery visits
Production up to 150,000 bottles

LA TORDERA
Via Alnè Bosco, 13, 31020 Vidor TV, Italia
+390423985362
info@latordera.it | www.latordera.it

Wine tastings, retail sales and winery visits
Production between 500,000 and 1,000,000 bottles

MASS BIANCHET
Via Soprapiana, 42, Vidor, TV, Italia
+393398277448
info@massbianchet.it | www.massbianchet.it

Wine tastings, retail sales, winery & vineyard visits
Production up to 150,000 bottles

MIOTTO Società Agricola
Via Scandolera, 24, Colbertaldo, TV, Italia
+390423985095
info@cantinamiotto.it | www.cantinamiotto.it

Wine tastings, retail sales, winery & vineyard visits
Production up to 150,000 bottles

The Miotto winery is a family business with several vineyards
spread throughout the Conegliano-Valdobbiadene area. They
produce 90,000 bottles of a stunning range of different Proseccos.

We had a short tasting (at our request) in a purpose-built tasting room, expertly hosted by Andrea, and tasted several DOCGs. I particularly enjoyed the Rive di Colbertaldo, a superb-tasting Prosecco.

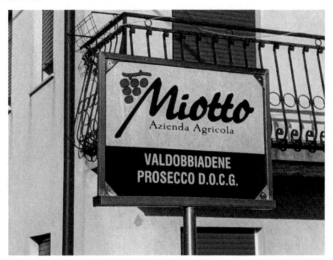

The Miotto winery

RICCARDO AZ. AGR. DI BOTTAREL FRANCESCA
via Cieca d'Alnè, 4 Vidor
+390423985248 | +390423989049
info@proseccoriccardo.com | www.proseccoriccardo.com

Open to the public, no further information given

SCANDOLERA soc agr snc
Via Scandolera, 95, Colbertaldo, TV, Italia
+390423985107 | +390423985107
info@scandolera.it | www.scandolera.it

Wine tastings, retail sales, winery visits
Production up to 150,000 bottles

SORELLE BRONCA

via Martiri della Liberazione, 20, Colbertaldo, Vidor
+300423987201 | 0423989329
info@sorellebronca.com | www.sorellebronca.com

Wine tastings, retail sales, accommodation, winery & vineyard visits
Production stated as between 100,000 and 500,000 bottles

I haven't visited the winery yet but bought Prosecco Brut to try at a tasting. Quite a fruity Prosecco with a persistent perlage.

SPAGNOL COL DEL SAS

Via Scandolera, 51, Vidor, 31020 TV, Italia
+390423987177 | +390423989100
info@spagnolcoldelsas.com | www.spagnolcoldelsas.com

Wine tastings, retail sales, and winery visits
Production stated as between 100,000 and 500,000 bottles

TORMENA F.lli

Via Roma, 208, 31020 Vidor TV, Italia
+390423987623 | +390423987623
tormenafratelli@libero.it | www.fratellitormena.it

Wine tastings, retail sales, and winery visits
Production up to 150,000 bottles

RIVACASELLE16

Farm RivaCaselle 16, Via Cornoler 16, B San Giovanni di Valdobbiadene, 31049 Treviso
+390423308325
info@rivacaselle16.com | rivacaselle16.com

Wine tastings, no further information given

Lunch in the vineyard

This winery is not listed on the Prosecco DOCG website but is definitely worth a look if you're in the area. Giulia arranged for a Prosecco lunch out in the vineyard, a beautiful setting where we ate and drank whilst learning more about the landscape and the lovely wines. I tried the Col Fondo; as you can see from the photo, this retains some yeast in the bottle and has a slightly cloudy appearance.

RivaCaselle Col Fondo

17. FARRA DI SOLIGO

Number of inhabitants: 8,704
Altitude: 163m
Area km²: 28.34
Patron Saint: Santo Stefano, Farra di Soligo – December 26;
Madonna of the Annunciation, Col San Martino – March 25;
Saints Peter and Paul, Soligo – 29 June

The first part of the name Farra Di Soligo probably derives from the Lombard FARA, or Germanic FARA, 'to go', typical of the region. The second part, officially added in 1867, derives from the name of one of its villages, which, in 1184, is shown as 'Suligo', derived from the Latin name of persona SULLA or SOLIUS, with the addition of the suffix -ICUS.

SS Pietro & Paolo

The village is a good central point for touring and has many picturesque pedestrian paths with the occasional picnic table, suitable for walkers and cyclists.

History

The municipality was founded by the Lombards around the 6th century. The town was consolidated in its modern form in 1806 from three original villages, Farra, Manchera and Credazzo. Rich in history, art and culture, the villages actually pre-date the year 1000. Each village had its own castle, all of which were destroyed around the 14th and 15th centuries; however, some traces remain, with Roman coins and mediaeval relics being found around the territory.

Other substantial findings have been uncovered in the area relating to the Lombard period. A burial site can be seen on the hill outside Manchera; it contained human remains with shields and other accoutrements and was unearthed in a pit between two cypress trees.

Original Lombard burial site

Feasts

Farra di Soligo hosts many Prosecco events, a selection of which are noted below:

<u>Valdobbiadene DOCG Exhibition</u> (www.prolococolsanmartino.it)

The Pro Loco Association organises and manages the oldest Prosecco DOCG exhibition, set up in the historic cellars of the Paccanoni family. The event is held in late March and early April and lasts three weeks, during which time all visitors have the opportunity to taste Prosecco DOCG and other locally produced wines, accompanied by typical local products such as sopressa, a type of salami. The exhibition hosts more than a hundred exhibitors representing the whole of the DOCG production area.

Locanda da Condo

<u>Vivi le Rive</u>

This is an annual Rive Vive walk, a unique sensorial trail winding through the hills above the Farra di Soligo area. Held at the end of May, it's a good opportunity to visit up to ten wineries and view historical sites from between the 10th and 14th centuries. There is an option of a couple of routes: both have Prosecco tasting opportunities and pairing with local breads, meats, cheeses and other typical local dishes prepared with the collaboration of restaurants.

Strawberry and Asparagus Festival (www.prolocofarra.it)

Organised by the Pro Loco Association of Farra di Soligo, this takes place towards the end of April.

Feast of Saints Peter and Paul (www.prolocosoligo.it)

Organised by the Pro Loco Association of Soligo, this festival takes place in late June on the patron saints' day. As part of this event, a local trade fair is arranged in which about 50 exhibitors from various product sectors participate.

Sun setting over Farra di Soligo

Market

The weekly market takes place on Tuesday mornings in Piazza Emigrante in Col San Martino.

Places of Interest

<u>Prosecco Safari</u>

I emailed to arrange a tasting visit at Le Volpere and was asked if I wanted to join a Prosecco safari. There's only one answer to that question! After receiving all the details for the event, I met our tour guide, Laura, and a party of fellow Prosecco thrill-seekers and we set off from the Church at Farra di Soligo just after 3pm.

Path at the start of Prosecco safari

We walked up an incline threading through rows of Prosecco vines, chatting as we went. After around 20 minutes' walk, we arrived at our first stop, visible in the photo above. Whilst this looks like a steep climb, we meandered through the vines and the walk wasn't quite as challenging as it looks. Villa Maria winery is situated on the main road in Farra di Soligo but they have an event space in the hills particularly for days such as this with a beautiful wooden balcony perched over the hillside, offering tremendous views over the area, where they serve some fabulous Prosecco and local meats and cheeses.

Villa Maria tasting table

After quenching our thirst and enjoying a selection of aperitifs, we set off for the next stop on our journey, another 20- to 30-minute walk up and down gently undulating hills to finally come to a rustic hut in the hills and a main course served with Le Volpere Prosecco. The guys were all set up, waiting for us with a table and seats in the vines, with lights to match. How lovely!

Path through the vines

Dinner ready at Le Volpere

An almost unexpected point on our walk took us to Le Volpere wine lodge, where we tried several luscious Proseccos whilst enjoying a hot lasagne as the evening drew in. After completely filling ourselves, we set off to walk the food off en route for our next winery.

Sun setting on Prosecco safari

We were advised to bring torches, although there was still plenty of light to get to our third and final stop at Lavinai Winery.

Typical Italian dessert awaited us as we approached in the last light of the day. This small winery is deep in the hills, although there is a road up to it. The tasting took place in the winery amongst the Prosecco tanks and again there was a great selection of Prosecco to try!

The countryside around Farra di Soligo has many tracks and trails suitable for walkers and hikers, as proved by our safari. Lush greenery accompanies your route and guides you up the hills to historic landmarks and epic views. Driving routes are available too.

Walking though the vines to our third stop

Lavinai winery in the hills

The route back to our starting point wasn't too arduous, as it was mostly downhill – but we did need our torches! Arriving back around 8pm, I had some sympathy for my fellow safari goers, who, after all the food we'd eaten, were booked in for a meal at 8.30 that evening.

The Towers of Credazzo

Along the hills above Farra di Soligo, the Towers of Credazzo can be seen. Unfortunately, this mediaeval complex is privately owned so can't be visited. The early structure was thought to have been built around the 9th or 10th century and was made up of a watch tower, a keep and a shielded tower spread over the area. Used as part of a defensive system incorporating other nearby castles, the towers have recently been restored.

One of the towers of Credazzo visible in the distance

The Hermitage of St Gallen

Originally the site of a castle held by the Da Caminos, it was raised to the ground in 1378 by Count Rambaldo di Collalto. The peaceful, isolated ruins gave way to a church built by Egidio di Lombardia, who saw the hermitage as a peaceful place of contemplation. The area is now a pilgrimage for insomniacs and legend states a splinter from the wooden cross placed under your pillow aids a restful night's sleep. The church stands at the top of the hill, shaded by cypress trees. It's a destination of beauty and serenity with fabulous views over the surrounding area.

St Gallen

Sanctuary of Collagù

From the small car park at the Hermitage of St Gallen, there is a hillside walk that takes you to the Sanctuary of Collagù. The ancient name was probably founded during the Bronze Age and is derived from the shape of the hill on which the sanctuary stands.

The legacy building was abandoned between the 18th and 19th centuries, being replaced in the 1930s. Consecrated in 1932, it is peaceful, isolated and silent and the resting place of the relics of Saint Emilio.

Air Force memorial

Villa Soligo

Villa Soligo is another of the many palaces and villas built by the Count of Brandolini in 1782 in the popular Palladian style. Two world wars took their toll on the villa; in WWII it was used as a garrison for German armed forces who set fire to the right wing on their retreat in 1944. It was subsequently restored by the Count but was only brought to its current state after a full restoration in 1980. Now a hotel, it has a peaceful existence and fabulous outlook.

Hotel Soligo

WINERIES

ADAMO CANEL sas
Via Castelletto, 73 31010 Farra di Soligo (TV)
+390438898112
info@adamocanel.it | www.canel.it

Wine tastings, retail sales
Production listed as up to 150,000 bottles

Adamo Canel tasting room is set up to the left of a very pretty, ornate Italian villa visible at the end of a long driveway. It was a busy Saturday lunchtime with an informal restaurant in the same area.

Ornately decorated Adamo Canel

They had a full suite of different wines, some local reds and whites as well as Brut and Extra Dry Prosecco. It's very central, so a visit can be undertaken without transport, and it is good to while away the afternoon sampling their range of stunning wines.

Wines and prosecco production of Adamo Canel

AZIENDA AGRICOLA ANDREOLA DI STEFANO POLA
Via Cavre, 19, Farra di Soligo, TV, Italia
+390438989379 | +390438898822
info@andreola.eu | www.andreola.eu

Wine tasting, retail sales, winery visits
Production between 500,000 and 1,000,000 bottles

I haven't visited this winery but their wine is available for sale in the UK. I held a tasting to sample one of their products. We tried the Rive di Refrontolo, Col del Forno, Brut. This was our favourite of the night: a full-bodied Prosecco, complex tasting with 7g of sugar. As it's at level 5 on the Prosecco pyramid of quality, I would have expected nothing less.

AZIENDA AGRICOLA BRANCHER SOCIETA' AGRICOLA S.S.

Via dei Prà, 23, Farra di Soligo, TV, Italia
+390438898227
mail@brancher.tv | www.brancher.tv

Wine tastings, retail sales
Production listed as up to 150,000 bottles

FOLLADOR PROSECCO

Via Gravette, 42, Col San Martino, TV, Italia
+390438898222 | +390438989520
info@folladorprosecco.com | www.folladorprosecco.com

Wine tasting, retail sales, winery & vineyard visits
Production between 500,000 and 1,000,000 bottles

Follador winery

LA FARRA
Via San Francesco, 44, Farra di Soligo, TV, Italia
+390438801242 | Fax +390438801504
info@lafarra.it | www.lafarra.it

Wine tastings, retail sales, winery & vineyard visits
Production between 100,000 and 500,000 bottles

LE RIVE DE NADAL Az. Agr.
Via dei Cavai, 42, Farra di Soligo, TV, Italia
+390438801315
info@lerivedinadal.com

No information listed

AZ.AGR. LE VOLPERE
via Ugo Cecconi, 13 Farra di Soligo
+390438801204
info@levolpere.it | www.levolpere.it

Wine tastings, retail sales, winery & vineyard visits
Production listed as up to 150,000 bottles

Having been introduced to Le Volpere during the Prosecco safari, I wanted to visit them at their winery and try several more of their fine selection of Prosecco. The 11-hectare vineyard and winery is run by two brothers, Matteo and Luca.

They're currently building a bigger tasting room for larger parties, which we had a look around. The room we were served in was absolutely fine, just at the side of the winery.

We tried an excellent Brut and a delicious Extra Brut with 0.5g of residual sugar. Hard to decide which I liked best!

Le Volpere extra brut prosecco

MARCHIORI
Via Rialto, 3, Farra di Soligo, TV, Italia
+390438801333
info@marchioriwines.com | www.marchioriwines.com

Wine tastings, retail sales, winery & vineyard visits
Production up to 150,000 bottles

MONGARDA
Via Canal Nuovo, 8, Farra di Soligo, TV, Italia
00390438989168
info@mongarda.it | www.mongarda.it

Wine tastings, retail sales, winery & vineyard visits
Production up to 150,000 bottles

Small winery with annual production of as little as 30,000 bottles.
They don't use herbicides or chemical fertilisers, instead using
green manure and compost to maintain the fertility of the soil.

MORO SERGIO AZ. AGR.
Via Crede, 10, Farra di Soligo, TV, Italia
+390438898381
info@morosergio.it | www.morosergio.it

No information about tastings or visits, although it does state it is open to the public
Production listed as up to 150,000 bottles

NARDI GIORDANO Az. Agr. "Soligo"
Via Piave, 13, Soligo, TV, Italia
+39043882458 | +390438985503
info@nardigiordano.com | www nardigiordano.com

Wine tastings, retail sales winery & vineyard visits
Production between 100,000 and 500,000 bottles

PERLAGE
Via Cal del Muner, 16, Farra di Soligo, TV, Italia
+390438900203
info@perlagewines.com | www.perlagewines.com

Wine tastings, retail sales, winery & vineyard visits.
Production between 100,000 and 500,000 bottles

CANTINA PROGETTIDIVINI
Via I Settembre, 20, Soligo, TV, Italia
+390438983151 | +390438837525
info@progettidivini.it | www.progettidivini.it

Wine tastings, retail sales, winery & vineyard visits.
Production between 100,000 and 500,000 bottles

RIVA GRANDA Soc Agr Ss
Via Canal Vecchio 5/a 31010 Col San Martino
+393334618684
info@proseccorivagranda.it | www.proseccorivagranda.it

Wine tastings, retail sales, sale of local food products, winery &
vineyard visits.
Production up to 150,000 bottles

Epic views at Riva Granda tasting

What a find this was! A sunny Sunday morning brought me to Silvia
at Riva Granda. The winery can be found at the edge of a residential
area and is walkable from the main road. You enter through a
courtyard where a small tasting room can be found; however, that
is not the experience you receive. Silvia took us up through the vines
to a clearing in the heart of the vineyard, with a rustic old farm
storage building, a specially set up tasting table and fabulous views
through the vines and towards the hills. It's optional whether you
walk up or are driven up, but it's well worth the visit. We sat in a
mixed group and sipped glasses of three very fine Proseccos with

tasting plates of cheese, bread and Silvia's homemade meats whilst she talked about the winery and the products. The labels on the bottles specify the area of the vineyard the grapes are taken from, which is a nice touch!

Light bites in the Riva Granda vineyard

RONFINI LEONARDO
Via del Prosecco, 7a. 31010 Col San Martino, TV, Italia
+390438989614
info@ronfini.com | www.ronfini.com

Wine tastings, retail sales, winery & vineyard visits
Production up to 150,000 bottles

SOC. AGR. SIRO MEROTTO S.S.
Via Castelletto, 88, Farra di Soligo, TV, Italia
+390438989156
info@siromerotto.it | www.siromerotto.it

Wine tastings, retail sales, winery & vineyard visits
Production up to 150,000 bottles

VILLA MARIA ss di Bevacqua di Panigai Rambaldo
Via S. Francesco, 28, 31010 Farra di Soligo TV, Italia
+390438801375 | +390438801121
info@villamaria-spumanti.it | www.villamaria-spumanti.it

Wine tastings, retail sales, winery visits
Production up to 150,000 bottles

This winery is very central. It's on the main road into Farra di Soligo, so is suitable if you don't have access to your own transport. They offer lovely, delicately-flavoured Prosecco and food to complement it.

Villa Maria lodge deep in the heart of the vineyard. Below: tasting table

18. PIEVE DI SOLIGO

Number of inhabitants: 12,047
Altitude: 185
Area km²: 19.02
Patron Saint: Santa Maria Maddalena – July 22

Pieve di Soligo is called 'the pearl of the Quartier del Piave' because of its pleasant geographical position in the amphitheatre of hills that border the area to the northeast. Pieve is thought to mean a neighbourhood in which a Christian community with a church and baptismal font was established.

The banks of the River Soligo can be accessed on foot or by bike and are ideal for relaxing walks and picturesque rides. The Lierza stream, which marks the border of the municipality with the neighbouring municipalities of Refrontolo and Susegana, also has some very interesting nature trails.

Vineyard

History

Whilst archaeological finds indicate a probable Roman settlement, like other neighbouring municipalities the centre of Pieve di Soligo is characterised by the presence of some interesting mediaeval buildings. Cal Santa is one of the oldest streets of the old town: it begins in the old village, just east of the parish church, and continues to the cemetery area, marked by Via Crucis. This street is the birthplace of Andrea Zanzotto, born in 1921 and one of the most famous 20th century Italian poets.

Located along the River Soligo is Borgo Stolfi, one of the historic villages of Pieve. It occupies the right bank of the river, near the parish church, where the river bends by the bridge. The architectural structures of the time are typical two- or three-storey buildings, according to the traditional style of villages of eastern Veneto. The old irrigation canal wheel mill, powered by the river, can also be found here.

Feasts

The village feast, Lo Spiedo Gigante, takes place on the first week of October. The highlight of the festival is the tug of war, traditionally held on the Soligo bridge with much celebration and flag waving, alongside traditional drummers and women dressed as maid servants. Sustenance is provided by the giant spit roast; quails are cooked for five to six hours over a fire of hornbeam and beech wood from the surrounding forests in a tradition dating back to 1956.

Places of Interest

Cathedral Church of Santa Maria Assunta

This is a substantial building, with roots dating back to 1192, found at the head of the Piazza Libertà. The old parish church was eventually demolished in 1924, being replaced with the rather beautiful interior of the cathedral church. The building, dedicated to Santa Maria Assunta, was designed by the architect Domenico Rupolo. The parish church houses an altarpiece representing the Assumption, by Francesco da Milano, and a sculpture by Marta Sammartini, one of the few 20th century female sculptresses, depicting the Virgin with the child Jesus. At the front of the church is a light-filled dome that sheds bright sunlight onto the altar.

Cathedral church of Santa Maria Assunta

Brandolino House

Villa Brandolini

This villa can be found off the same square, Piazza Libertà. The 18th century Venetian style villa was purchased by the town in 1977 and, as the Francesco Fabbri Culture Centre, is the venue for many cultural events, concerts and art exhibitions. It is the headquarters of the Consortium Tutela Prosecco Doc of Conegliano Valdobbiadene, the Toti Dal Monte Music Association and the Toti Dal Monte Museum offices.

Notable Locals

Andrea Zanzotto was born in 1921 in Pieve, living there for the majority of his life. He is known for being one of the most significant poets of Italy, author of works that have become fundamental in the landscape of 20th century literature. He died in Conegliano in 2011.

WINERIES

Soc. Agr. BALLANCIN LINO s.s.
Via Drio Cisa, 11, Solighetto, TV, Italia
+390438842749
viniballancin@viniballancin.com | www.viniballancin.com

Wine tasting, retail sales, winery & vineyard visits
Production of up to 150,000 bottles

CANTINA COLLI DEL SOLIGO
Via Lino Toffolin, 6, Pieve di Soligo, TV, Italia
+390438840092 | +39043882630
comunicazione@collisoligo.com | www.collisoligo.com

Wine tasting, retail sales, sale of local food products, winery visits
Production of over 1,000,000 bottles

Cantina Colli del Soligo

Sales are conducted in the local wine shop, which can't be missed as it's set within a large car park off the main road. It's a lovely browsing area but it closes at lunchtime, so take that into consideration.

Az Agr di SCOTTA EVANGELISTA
Via Fabbri Francesco, 150, Solighetto, TV, Italia
+393475973489
info@cantinascotta.it | www.cantinascotta.it

Open to the public, no further information given

19. SUSEGANA

Number of inhabitants: 11,780
Altitude: 76
Area km²: 44.10
Patron Saint: Santa Maria Ausiliatrice – May 24

The municipality of Susegana is thought to date back to the Bronze Age. It is likely the toponym of Susegana dates back to the Roman colonisation of the Piave valley and would refer to the name of the owner of a plot (Sosus or Sosius). Like several other municipalities, it includes the Roman-built Via Claudia Augusta, allowing easy access from the Adriatic through to Bavaria and the Danube.

Susegana

History

After the fall of the western Roman Empire, the territory suffered from a succession of Barbarian invasions until the arrival of the

Lombards, giving rise to the long history of the Collalto family in the area. It was thanks to the Lombards, and to their knowledge and experience in terms of the strategic and military importance of the zone, that Susegana and its surrounding area was able to promote trade activities successfully. At the same time, the population remained extremely well protected and defended, with the result that the area attracted settlements of various kinds, including monastic foundations.

The favourable position, a natural place of transit between the Venetian Prealps, the Piave river, the rich foothills and the great alluvial plain, made Collalto a commercial centre in pre-Roman times. It still retains its imagery as a mediaeval hamlet and is home to the ruins of what was the first Collalto seat in the Piave region. Built in 1110, Collalto Castle was constructed to guard the ford over the Piave river. The imposing guard tower of the original castle still rises above the ruins of its three impregnable surrounding walls.

Following the construction of a second castle, the more impressive Castle of San Salvatore, Collalto Castle fell out of favour, being used solely as a defensive structure. It was used as a monastery until Napoleonic times and was eventually a silk mill, taking advantage of the area's production.

This area suffered severe destruction during the Battle of Caporetto. The castle was used by the occupation forces, and was later bombarded by Italian artillery, severely damaging the structure and causing the destruction of many works of art. The town was regenerated after WWII and is now home to numerous cultural initiatives promoted by the small but active local community. There is a popular walk with several different routes, starting from Susegana Square, rising to the castle of San Salvatore and continuing towards Colle della Tombola until it reaches the hamlet of Collalto, where the ruins of Collalto Castle can be seen. Alternatively, a gentle amble along the left bank of the Piave may suit the less ambitious; it passes marked WWI sites and travels along the side of ancient Roman bridges.

Collalto Castle (photograph courtesy of Sui Colle)

The Legend of Bianca di Collalto

In mediaeval times, infighting between powerful local families was often settled with a marriage, as was the case between Tolberto di Collalto and Chiara da Camino, two leading families of Lombard origin. The union was not a happy one, with Tolberto choosing a life as a soldier to avoid living with his morbidly jealous wife. Bianca di Collalto attended Chiara as her personal maid but broke down in tears on hearing the Count was leaving for war. The jealous Chiara interpreted the outburst as a sign of her husband's infidelity and, despite the young maid's protestations of innocence, Chiara punished her by walling her up alive in a tower. The count only became aware of this on his return and evicted his wife from the castle. Legend states Bianca remains at the castle and her ghostly apparition appears to the family before happy events or a great disaster. Those who claim to have seen the ghost say that Bianca usually appears in white to announce happy news and with a black veil in front of her face to announce a misfortune.

Feasts

Vino in Villa, the Conegliano Valdobbiadene DOCG International Festival

Vino in Villa is an annual international festival to celebrate the new Conegliano-Valdobbiadene DOCG denomination. The rooms and gardens of the Castle of San Salvatore are open to the public for the traditional tasting with tasting stands. It's held annually one Sunday in May.

Market

The weekly market takes place every Wednesday morning in the square and includes a farmer's market.

Places of Interest

Castle of San Salvatore

The castle of San Salvatore was founded, built and is still owned by the Collalto family, of ancient Lombard lineage. Construction first began in 1323 by Rambaldo VIII. This and the castle of Collalto were ancient feudal seats from which the family could demonstrate their considerable power and prestige.

Castle of San Salvatore

As with most castles, its situation was not by chance. With an imposing view over the surrounding area, it was gradually adapted and reinforced, becoming one of the most fortified palaces in Europe. But it also served as an area of culture, drawing writers, poets and artists. The famous painter Cima da Conegliano used the castle and surroundings as a background for many of his famous works. The family also became famed for hosting large and sumptuous events. Count Antonio IV hosted over 4,000 guests for the wedding of his daughter, Matilda, with tournaments, jousting and days of revelry.

WINERIES

BERNARDI PIETRO Az. Agr. S.S.
Via Mercatelli Sant'Ana, Susegana, TV, Italia
+390438781022 | +390438781022
info@bernardivini.com | www.bernardivini.com

Wine tasting, retail sales
Production listed as between 100,000 and 500,000 bottles

BORGOLUCE
Località Musile, 2, Susegana, TV, Italia
+390438435287
info@borgoluce.it | www.borgoluce.it

Wine tasting, accommodation, restaurant, retail sales, sale of local
products, winery & vineyard visits
Production listed as between 100,000 and 500,000 bottles

COL SANDAGO
Via Barriera, 41, Susegana, TV, Italia
+39043864468 | +390438453871
info@colsandago.it | www.colsandago.it

Wine tasting, retail sales, winery visits
Production between 100,000 and 500,000 bottles

CONTE COLLALTO
Via XXIV Maggio, 1, Susegana, TV, Italia
+390438435811
info@cantine-collalto.it | www.cantine-collalto.it

Wine tastings, accommodation, retail sales, winery & vineyard
visits

Collalto winery

MALIBRAN
Via Barca II 63 31058, Susegana
+390438781410
info@malibranvini.it | www.malibranvini.it

Wine tastings, retail sales, winery & vineyard visits
Production up to 150,000 bottles

TENUTA ZAGO GASPARINI

Via Cucco, Susegana, TV, Italia
+393428213053
commerciale@zagogasparini.com | 2castelli.com

Wine tastings, Accommodation, E-commerce, retail sales, winery
& vineyard visits
Production up to 150,000 bottles

TERRE BOSCARATTO

Via Ponte Vecchio 5/a, Susegana, TV, Italia
+3904381736690
info@terreboscaratto.com | www.terreboscaratto.com

Wine tastings, Accommodation, E-commerce, retail sales, winery
& vineyard visits
Production up to 150,000 bottles

VALDELLOVO S.S. DI RICCI B & C SOC AGR

Via Antonio Gramsci, 4/c, Susegana, TV, Italia
+390438981232 | +390438738619
info@valdellovo.it | www.valdellovo.it

Wine tastings, retail sales & winery visits
Production up to 150,000 bottles

20. ASOLO

Number of inhabitants: 9,068
Altitude: 200m
Area km²: 25.37
Patron Saint: San Prosdocimo – November 7

Asolo is a town and municipality known as 'the pearl of the province of Treviso'. Encompassing more than 30 villages and hamlets, the favourable position and the climate ensures Asolo has been an inhabited centre since pre-historic times. It's a fabulous, fashionable, well-heeled kind of place, with frescoed, arched walkways on the streets housing specialist shops and delicatessens, small eateries and local commerce. Defined by Giosuè Carducci as the city of a hundred horizons, Asolo is one of the most characteristic historical centres in Italy. It retains evidence of its history in every glimpse. It's a place of charm and inspiration for poets and writers, artists and travellers, who found creative harmony in this place of natural beauty. A sense of history and tradition pervades every street corner, from the many and beautiful villas and ornate private residences to its legacy castle.

Truly beautiful in its situation, surrounded by lush green vegetation and ancient forests, it has been a magnet for painters and poets and still draws famous personalities to partake of its cool persona. The Castle of Queen Cornaro, together with the Rocca, one of the symbols of the Asolan landscape, date back to the 10th century; it was the home of the Venetian podestàs, and Caterina Cornaro, Queen of Cyprus, Jerusalem and Armenia, Lady of Asolo from 1489 to 1510.

Asolo creeps up on you and is well worth a visit. The smells and flavours of local products, the taste of good food, the artisan shops that, together with taverns and cafes, overlook porches and squares are part of the persuasive ambience that you can feel as you walk through the streets of the town. The atmosphere is enhanced by the possibility of a stop in a wine shop and the aromas from the eateries in the narrow mediaeval streets. It is still possible to find bread baked in wood and artisanal shops with local salami, wines, grappas, oils, jams and delicious desserts. Local products are available: artisanal cheeses such as Morlacco and Bastardo, Grappa oil, Maser cherries and Grappa honey. Restaurants and trattorias, like most things in Asolo, are elegant places where you can enjoy dishes derived from superb local produce: from sardines in saor to bigoli in sauce, from mushroom soups to pasta and beans, or Castelfranco radicchio, pumpkin and Bassano white asparagus.

View from the castle

Try the typical 'cicchetti' accompanied by a glass of Prosecco Asolo DOCG, or delicious specialties such as elderberry ice cream or 'Tintoretto', a variant of Bellini with pomegranate. It is not difficult to imagine the famous people who have stayed in this city over the past two centuries strolling through the town, chatting with locals or enjoying a morning coffee, from poets or musicians such as Robert Browning and Gian Francesco Malipiero to celebrities like Mastroianni, La Deneuve, Yoko Ono and many others.

As with all regions of Italy, Asolo has both local and historic grapes and a proliferation of wines: vigorous reds and flavoursome whites such as Merlot, Cabernet, Prosecco, Chardonnay, Pinot and Manzoni, along with the elegant Prosecco Superiore. Asolo is the centre of the Montello and Colli Asolani DOC production, and the best selections have received many national and international awards.

Feasts

Antiques Market

Held every second Sunday of the month. Furniture, jewellery, silverware, prints and books, modern antiques and objects in general are exhibited along the streets of the historic centre.

Calici di Stelle

This is included in the national circuit of the wine cities, every August as in other Italian wine cities, and the best local wines and typical local products are celebrated with tastings.

Places of Interest

There is much to see in Asolo. Whether you're an architectural history buff or a gourmet food connoisseur, both appetites can be filled with a walk around the town and the surrounding area. There are plenty of historic buildings with stories of their legacies, all individual. Asolo is such a fantastic place to wander around. As in other chapters, I've not listed all its famous buildings and churches; should you wish to find more places of interest, I would suggest you contact the local tourist information office in Asolo. Following is a selection of historic landmarks that you might like to view during your visit.

The Rocca

This military fortress has links back to the 6th-9th centuries, when it was thought to be an early religious building with a large cemetery. A piece of the highly patterned mosaic floor from the original building, depicting early Christian symbols, is preserved in the civic museum in Asolo. The fortification was built between the late 12th and early 13th centuries, serving as a garrison for the city. Its commanding position assured the early occupants surety from attack, with epic views around the whole of the surrounding area from the Dolomites to Venice.

The Rocca seen in the background on the hill

Archaeological investigations conducted in the 1990s by the University of Padua reconstructed the history of the fortification, presenting several successive stages of settlement and causing a much-required restoration. An important feature of the restoration was to ensure the practicability of the patrol path, accessed via a staircase in order to view the surrounding landscape and its interior. Interesting remains of accommodation with wooden floors and brick hearths date back to the 15th century, together with documents for the supply of weapons and provisions that testify to the strategic importance of the fortress at that time.

The City Walls

Most mediaeval settlements were hotly contested and Asolo was no different, with continuous struggles between Verona, Padua and the Serenissima Republic. The geographical position of Asolo allowed for the building of city walls to protect it from these attacks and a defence structure was built in the 14th century around the urban perimeter, extending up to the Rocca on top of Monte Ricco, with 24 towers arranged at strategic points along the drystone walls. Some sections have since fallen in decay.

City walls

Civic Museum

The museum occupies the annexed Palazzo del Vescovado and the building of the Loggia della Ragione, former palace of the municipality in the 14th century. The façade has a fresco decoration from 1588 depicting the defeat of Crassus against the Parthians, whilst in the north-facing part of the attic, cartouches and vegetable festoons can be seen. It houses personal artefacts of local inhabitants such as Eleanor Duse and Robert Browning.

Asolo Castle

Also known as Caterina Cornaro Castle, Asolo Castle can be found at the southwest part of the city centre and dominates as a local landmark. It's not known when it was built; however, it is referenced in a document of 969 decreeing the end of the diocese of Asolo. It was incorporated into the city walls for fortification and became home to Caterina Cornaro in 1489, where she welcomed painters, poets and writers. After the Queen's death in 1510, the building underwent modifications and restoration ranging from the 17th to the 19th centuries.

Asolo castle

Napoleon used the castle as accommodation for troops and in WWI it became a prison. On the walls there are charcoal drawings made by the detained soldiers. Subsequently, two towers were reduced in height whilst the majestic bell, or civic tower, is still clearly visible from every corner of the city; of the original four, only three towers remain today. In the castle courtyard there is an open-air space, which is used for summer events, and two of the castle towers – the

Reata and Civic towers – are open to the public at weekends and give panoramic views around the countryside.

Duse Theatre

The Great Hall in the castle was transformed in 1798 into a stable theatre by the Italian impresario Antonio Locatelli. In the 1950s, the theatre was purchased by the State of Florida, dismantled and shipped to Sarasota, where it can be seen in the John & Mable Ringling Museum of Art. The only reminder of the old theatre is the crystal chandelier that now illuminates the Council Hall of the Town Hall.

Fontana Maggiore

Until the early 20th century, the Fontana Maggiore was the main system of water collection in the centre of town, thanks to the supply of underground aqueducts thought to be part of original Roman baths.

Archaeological Park Garden of Villa Freya

The house and gardens found at the Portello di Castelfranco were the home of Lady Freya Stark, the great English traveller and writer who made her home in Asolo. Now a botanical garden, accessed only by appointment, it houses plants and essences brought back from her regular trips to the Middle East. Reference to her love of the Middle East and her multilingual work can be seen on the access door to the house, where an oriental-style ceramic tile with Arabic inscription sits.

The Mallet Workshop

Dating back to the 15th century, the mallet workshop was originally used for metalworking and is situated by the canal, bordered at right angles to the house to form a courtyard. The interior of the workshop encompasses two water wheels, two grinding wheels, a large mallet and two pairs of bellows; a set of tools that seems to indicate well-established and consolidated activity. In the 17th century, the complex changed functional use, becoming a saw mill. It returned to its original purpose in the 19th century as a blacksmith's, no doubt necessary for shoeing the horses of Napoleon's men. The house was registered to the Colla family and remained in their hands until very recently. Visiting is allowed.

Fontana Maggiore

Asolo centre

Notable Locals

Three women, Caterina Cornaro, Eleonora Duse and Freya Stark enjoyed an intense bond with Asolo. Intrepid, uncompromising women in their own right, they continued to promote Asolo as an ideal of beauty and place of choice. Whilst they travelled extensively, they returned often and spent a great deal of their lives here. Between the 19th and 20th centuries, Asolo affirmed its character as a place of beauty and cultural tradition, attracting intellectuals and artists, both Italian and foreign: among them Eugene Benson, Henry James and Carlo Scarpa, Marius Pictor, Filippo De Pisis, Igor Stravinsky and Ernest Hemingway.

Caterina Cornaro was born in 1454 in the Palazzo di San Cassiano, Venice. Her parents were the noble knight Marco Cornaro and Fiorenza Crespo. The family of Cornaro were wealthy traders, with much of their wealth coming from Cyprus, where various branches of the family owned large estates and plantations. Her uncle, Andrea, proposed a marriage for Caterina to the King of Cyprus, offering the advantage of a marriage bond with a daughter from Venice. After being 'adopted' by the city, Catherine reached her husband on the island in 1472, where she was crowned 'Queen of Cyprus, Jerusalem and Armenia'. After the death of her husband, King James, Caterina Cornaro was appointed to rule Cyprus until 1489 when, for Venetian aims, she was forced to surrender the kingdom to the Serenissima Republic in exchange for dominion over the land of Asolo.

She lived in Asolo Castle, which had become a meeting place for artists and illustrious personalities. After spending her last years between Asolo and the palaces of Venice, in 1510 the queen died in the Palazzo di San Cassiano.

Eleanora Duse (Vigevano 1858-Pittsburgh 1924). Duse, as she became known, was a famous Italian actress who attracted fans such as James Joyce, Anton Chekhov, Henrik Ibsen and Charlie Chaplin. The first woman to be featured on *Time* magazine, Duse came from inauspicious beginnings; her early life was spent in abject poverty, where she was often reduced to begging. She learnt to read from scripts and was thrown into acting because her family were touring actors; she often appeared on stage with them.

By the middle of the 1880s, Duse came to be regarded as Italy's greatest actress and performed many of the roles also played by her contemporary and great rival, Sarah Bernhardt. While Bernhardt enjoyed the greater popularity, portraying her roles with elaborate stage make-up and costuming, it seems that Duse's more stripped back approach brought her more critical success.

After a failed marriage to the actor Tebaldo Marchetti (aka Tebaldo Checchi), with whom she had a daughter, Enrichetta, she had a long-term relationship with the Italian playwright and poet Gabriele D'Annunzio. Plagued with ill health, she quit the stage in 1909 but worked on the film *Cenere*. Not content in retirement, she returned to the stage in 1921, appearing in London, Vienna and New York. She died on tour in the US but is buried in Asolo.

Freya Stark (Paris 1893-Asolo 1993) – what a woman! Born of unconventional, liberal-minded parents, she was brought up in Italy and England. Exposed to several languages as a child, along with riding and mountaineering, she developed an early thirst for adventure. She attacked life with a certain amount of gusto and aplomb, along with a can-do attitude. During WWI, she broke off her studies to become a nurse in Italy, also spending time working as a censor for international correspondence.

With a deep fascination of the Middle East, she learned Arabic to allow her to travel, journeying to Lebanon in 1927. Subsequent trips enabled her to develop her understanding of the people, language and customs. She travelled from Damascus to Baghdad, where she associated with diplomats and locals in equal measure, enjoying desert excursions to meet Bedouin tribes and totally ignoring the moral codes for women. Her next trip would be to Persia, where she undertook mapping out the archaeological details of the Valleys of the Assassins, receiving serious recognition in colonial circles and a reputation as an explorer. Further trips ensued, covering Kurdistan, Persia, Yemen, Egypt, Iraq and India, where she was able to satisfy her curiosity, map out new territories and live among the locals, gaining worthwhile insight into their nature, mentality and customs. She spent the majority of WWII in the Middle East as an advisor to the British colonial administration.

She returned to Asolo, where she'd spent time as a child. She enjoyed time writing books about her experiences and continued to plan trips abroad, learning Turkish and studying history to equip herself for further travels continuing into her eighties, with trips to Persia, Afghanistan and Iraq. She lived to be over 100, spending the last years of her life in Asolo.

Robert Browning (London 1812-Venice 1889), the famous British poet and playwright, travelled extensively throughout Italy; his first trip, in 1838, was to study the setting for his poem, *Sordello*. After several visits he settled in Florence with his wife, the poet Elizabeth Barrett, and used his Italian experiences as the inspiration for many more of his famous works. He had a real connection to Asolo and visited many times, dedicating one of his poems, *Asolando*, to Caterina Bronson, a native of Asolo. He died in Venice on 12 December 1889.

City living

WINERIES

Asolo gained Prosecco DOCG recognition later than the Conegliano-Valdobbiadene Consortium and was added to the Prosecco DOCG, identifying itself with the labelling of Asolo Prosecco DOCG. The consortium is the Consorzio Vini Asolo Montello; it covers 19 municipalities and also includes Montello DOCG – a red wine. I've not visited any of the Asolo wineries to date. Some of the wineries in this DOCG area also feature in the Conegliano-Valdobbiadene area depending on their vineyards.

VILLA DI MASER Az. Agr. Di Diamante Luling Buschetti
Via Cornuda, 7, 31010 Maser, TV, ITALIA
+39 0423 923003
Telefax: +39 0423 923002
wine@villadimaser.it | www.villadimaser.it

Retail sales, wine tastings
No further information given

Prosecco from Villa Di Maser is included in the Montello and Colli Asolani DOC. The villa is described in fuller detail in the Surrounding Areas chapter. If you're planning a visit, I would advise arriving before lunch so you can enjoy the wonderful food at the adjoining restaurant and bar area. They do tastings of Prosecco and other wines from their winery and have a shop selling local produce. There's nothing better than sitting in the

sunshine, enjoying fine food and being educated on the local produce! Check the opening days and times before setting off.

Lunch outside the old stables – Villa di Maser

VILLA SANDI

Via Erizzo, 112 Crocetta del Montello, TV, Italia
+39 0423 665009
info@villasandi.it | www.villasandi.it

Accommodation, restaurant, wine tasting, retail sales, wine &
vineyard visits
Production over 1,000,000 bottles

Villa Sandi is a well-known producer of Prosecco at different levels,
brands and grades and is included in the Prosecco DOCG
consortium. There is a wonderful, well-maintained building, a sight
to behold and a fine example of a very typical Italian villa. The
adjoining wine shop sells their fabulous Prosecco alongside local
wines and other beautifully packaged gifts.

Villa Sandi

They offer various tastings and tours of the villa; tastings commence
in one of the many vaulted ceiling cellars, all lined with ancient oak
barrels and rack upon rack of wine. The multi-coloured crystal

chandeliers in the villa are original and whilst the rooms aren't fully furnished, the tour includes a view of the sculptured gardens, a collection of motorbikes and a corridor full of moose heads!

Villa Sandi tour

One of the many Villa Sandi cellars

CIROTTO WINERY by Cirotto Giovanni & C.

Via Bassanese, 51, Asolo, TV, Italia
+39 0423 952396
info@cirottovini.com | www.cirottovini.com

I've not visited this winery but I have sampled their Prosecco. They were the first winery I'd heard of selling Extra Brut Prosecco, and it has a very low sugar content. Well established, they have a fine selection of Prosecco and their cellar/shop is open daily.

No further information is given.

~~~

As mentioned earlier, Asolo is part of the Consorzio Vini Asolo Mondello, a different consortium, not included in the basis of this book, which is why I've only included a small selection.

There are many other wineries that are part of the Consorzio Vini Asolo Montello, should you wish to visit. Based predominantly around Asolo and the surrounding area, you will find their details on the Consortium's website.

21. SURROUNDING AREA

The Prosecco area has its fair share of castles, villas and impressive mediaeval churches; however, if you have sufficient time you might want to include some attractions from around the surrounding region. The following sites are each notable in their own right for being either a place of grandeur, of stillness and tranquillity, or of great historic value, some of them all three.

Bassano del Grappa

The characteristic Ponte degli Alpini, the 16th century Mannerist painter Jacopo Bassano, and ceramic production are the symbols that give this town its international notoriety. The Ponte degli Alpini (the 16th century wooden bridge designed by Andrea Palladio), the Castello degli Ezzelini, the Civic Museum and numerous frescoed buildings embellish the historic centre. Mediaeval testimonies mingle with Venetian architecture within the three city walls, which mark the urban development of Roman origins. Cultural life is full of events, shows and exhibitions. The pedestrian path along the city walls offers a splendid view of the foothills and the entire city.

Bassano is particularly well known for its Grappa. Made from leftovers of the winemaking process, the fiery liqueur can be found all over Italy. One of Bassano's historic distilleries, Poli, hosts the Museo della Grappa in its headquarters, where you can learn how Grappa is made and taste it too. Admission is free and the museum is open all day.

The town centre is comprised of pretty streets, three attractive linked piazzas, the 15th century town hall, various small cafes and interesting shops. The Giardini Parolini, a botanical garden created by a local enthusiast in the early 19th century, is a beautiful public park.

Bassano is dominated by the Castello degli Ezzelini. The courtyards are open but the castle itself can only be visited by prior arrangement.

Mount Grappa – The Mausoleum

The memorial on top of Mount Grappa was built in 1935 to honour the fallen of the First World War. The monument is comprised of two parts: the central body, where the remains of 12,615 Italian soldiers are kept, and the 250m long 'Way of Heroes', where the battles are recorded. The basement of the central building is made of five 4m-high concentric circles separated from each other by a 10m-wide level corridor. It ends in 'Portale Roma', where the observatory was built. On the balcony, you will find a bronze plan showing the various battlefields and the battlefront in June 1918.

Antonio Canova Museum

Antonio Canova Museum

Although he was born in Possagno, the unquestioned representative of Italian neoclassical sculpture, Antonio Canova (1757-1822) spent most of his life in Rome, where he settled in 1781. An incredible parade of his complete collection of works is visible in Possagno in the house where he was born, where you can linger in front of his canvases, drawings and portraits. The Gipsoteca demonstrates his working methods, starting from an initial sketch, through wax to a clay model, creating a mould for the plastercast model, which enabled him to pin the proportions down for the finished piece. He took prestigious commissions, including one from the first US president, George Washington. Other exhibits of his work are displayed all over the world, including at Chatsworth House and in Edinburgh and New York.

Canova Sculpture found in Chatsworth House

Take a walk up the tree-flanked avenue that starts from the centre of Possagno and leads to the colossal temple, designed and built by Canova himself and consecrated in 1832 as the parish church of Possagno, where the artist was buried after his death.

Canova mausoleum

View from the mausoleum / temple roof

The dome, a perfect hemisphere, rests on a circular golden frieze and is artistically decorated. The floor is made using white and red marble from the Piave river, whilst the side altar houses paintings by great Italian masters: Luca Giordano, Palma the Young, Andrea

Vicentino and Il Pordenone. The altarpiece of the temple depicts the Trinity (Deposition of Christ) by Canova as the ultimate tribute to his everlasting genius.

Villa di Maser, also known as Villa Barbaro

Villa di Maser (as mentioned in the previous chapter), aka Villa Barbaro, was built between 1550 and 1560 for the brothers Daniele and Marcantonio Barbaro. It is considered one of the highest examples of the genius of Andrea Palladio. The villa was born from an unusual and extraordinary collaboration between the designer and the clients – refined lovers and connoisseurs of classical architecture. Villa and landscape merge together and it is one of the most astonishing examples of 16th century Venetian culture and lifestyle.

Villa di Maser / Villa Barbaro

Built in a slightly elevated position, the gardens are accessed by both floors. Internal decoration was carried out by Paolo Veronese, who painted the frescoes, and Alessandro Vittoria, who was responsible for the stuccos. The building opens towards the plain, briefly interrupted by the public road before continuing in the scenic tree-lined avenue that extends indefinitely towards the horizon. In line with the public road, a few metres from the villa, the Tempietto was built in 1580, the last work of Palladio. Built on the classical theme of the Roman Pantheon, it was the only opportunity offered to Palladio to build a church in a 'round shape', which he considered ideal for sacred buildings. On the hill behind the villa you can visit the curious 'Carriage Museum'.

I love to visit this site, and do so regularly, particularly for lunch at the old farmhouse alongside the villa. Visitors can take some light refreshments or a superb lunch, along with guided wine tastings, course by course.

Villa Emo

A fundamental stop for Palladian enthusiasts is in Fanzolo di Vedelago for the Villa Emo-Capodilista. A part of Palladio's UNESCO World Heritage Site, it was built between 1557 and 1560 for the noble Emo family and remained in their possession through the centuries until 2005.

Villa Emo

The design, which has a high centre but is built in a unique linear structure, was the first of its kind and makes the palace look bigger and more opulent. Whilst the façade is simple classical style, it is furnished inside with incredible marble floors, pieces of period furniture and heraldry; some fabulous opulent frescoes ensure story-telling around each room, including the depiction of an awe-inspiring world of mythological figures and amazing landscapes.

San Vito di Altivole – Brion Tomb

Located in San Vito di Altivole, the Brion Tomb represents one of the most interesting funeral monuments of modern architecture. It was built in the early 1970s by the famous architect Carlo Scarpa on behalf of the Brion family.

Brion Tomb

The work is characterised by one of the typical elements of Scarpa's work: water, used as a metaphor for the perennial flow of life. The serene atmosphere of the place makes it seem like an oriental garden rather than a funeral site.

The tombs of the two Brions are inclined towards each other to indicate the union of the two people. It plays on the harmony of the differing materials of concrete, wood and metal.

Treviso

It would be remiss to highlight places worthy of a visit outside of the
Conegliano-Valdobbiadene area without mentioning Treviso. It is
often compared unfavourably with its noble counterpart, Venice,
but I think Venice can sometimes be a little overwhelming with its
fast-paced style, endless tourists and the busy atmosphere, whereas
Treviso is a pleasant, well-preserved and compact city, respectful of
its past whilst remaining slightly understated and a lot less manic.

The history of Treviso is depicted in its marvellous frescoed villas
and quiet canals, where Europe's longest resurgent river, the Sile,
flows past the 16th century city walls. Like many of its neighbours,
Treviso has undergone several dominations through the centuries
Traditionally a Lombard stronghold, it was fought over and won by
different feuding knights until the remainder of the area passed to
the Venetian Republic, eventually joining the remaining Italian
strongholds and becoming part of a unified Italy in 1860.

Treviso

The town is a rambling maze of streets lined with arcaded walkways; its defensive walls, moat and imposing gateways are still impressive sights. Treviso is home to the clothing empire Benetton, which has its flagship store on the city's smartest street, the Via Calmaggiore, which stretches from Piazza dei Signori towards the Duomo, between the beautiful arcaded streets. Unlike Venice, this town doesn't depend on tourism – you won't find a plethora of tourist shops, tourist fayre or tour guides; just a well-heeled Italian town going about its daily business.

The town's civic heart is the spacious Piazza dei Signori, boasting plenty of shops, cafés and eateries. It's a lovely place, with an air of prosperity, and worth a visit to walk around and admire its pleasant buildings and try a little local retail therapy.

22. MY PICKS

As you can see, there are hundreds of wineries to choose from. I've visited the area many times over the last seven years and I'm still discovering new wineries on each trip. On my visits I'm torn between visiting old friends and exploring new wineries and, depending on my fellow travellers, I try to do a mix of the two.

Most trips I make are three-day, two-night stays. This allows you sufficient time to see the area, enjoy the landscape, eat at a couple of choice restaurants and sample some very fine Prosecco. My recommendation would be to plan in advance and book the tastings you'd like to do before you arrive in the area. Be clear what you would like from the tasting – whether it is a winery tour or a simple tasting, how many Proseccos you'd like to sample, and, if food is available, whether you'd like to incorporate lunch. Don't try to do too many; it would be rather overwhelming. I would suggest two or possibly three a day, maximum.

A lot of hotel booking websites will give you available options. I've also listed some wineries that can provide accommodation. My own personal favourite is the family hotel with pool in Pedeguarda, just outside Follina. For me, it's a little piece of paradise!

Hotel Villaguarda Landscape Experience

Things to watch out for:

- A lot of the wineries close for lunch, which can be anytime between 12 and 2pm.
- August is a holiday period in Italy and some wineries close for a week or two before the harvest season.
- September is harvest time. Traffic is slightly heavier with all the tractors transporting grapes, and the winery staff will be extremely busy so might not be able to accommodate you.

A sample trip (incorporating my absolute favourite wineries) could look something like this.

Day 1

Morning

Whether you arrive mid-morning or enjoy a relaxing breakfast, for those who travelled the evening before, you could spend time visiting the castle in Conegliano, or taking a drive to Tarzo to see the lakes, or to the Molinetta della Croda, the ancient waterwheel, which is quite close to the Toffoli winery.

Afternoon

2pm   Toffoli Prosecco, Refrontolo.

The best introduction! Sante will show you the whole production and bottling process before producing several fantastic bottles of Prosecco, along with meats and cheeses for you to try. He will always ask if you'd like to try the other great wines he produces and you'll find yourself indulging in several local red and white wines. Sante has great, up to date knowledge of the area and is interesting and interested. He's recently started selling other products such as tea towels, aprons, baseball caps etc. It's likely to be the only place you can purchase these items, so make sure you make the most of it.

4pm   Riva Granda Prosecco, Farra di Soligo.

It's a superb environment to drink Prosecco. Silvia will drive you into the hills of the vineyard where you'll be greeted by spectacular views in a rustic tasting area. You'll try three different Proseccos accompanied by local meats and cheeses, all served up overlooking those epic views.

Table set at Riva Granda

<u>Evening</u>

Depending on where you are staying, you could try La Fucina Restaurant in Castelbrando for the evening meal. It's a relaxed place, serving pizza and other local dishes. Entrance to Castelbrando for non-residents is via the funicular railway. You will need two euros each for the return journey.

Castle for dinner?

Day 2

Start day two with a relaxing morning by the pool or, for the more adventurous, try a drive over to Asolo to amble through the town, browse some exquisite shops and admire the views from the castle whilst enjoying the atmosphere – depending on where you are staying, of course.

Or maybe visit Possagno, to see the museum and mausoleum of Antonio Canova, the famous sculptor. You can walk over the dome of the mausoleum (not for the faint-hearted!). There's a lovely patisserie by the museum for a coffee and cake stop.

Cake anyone?

Afternoon

2pm   Terre di San Venanzio, Valdobbiadene.

Now you've become a Prosecco connoisseur, it's time to try one of the fabulous award-winning Proseccos. Have a tasting with Monica and try the demi-long Prosecco, served in exquisite glasses; it's my favourite. This is also an opportunity to contrast it with Prosecco from Asolo, from a separate consortium and area.

The stunning Brut Cartizze at Terre di San Venanzio

4pm   San Gregorio
Prosecco, Valdobbiadene.

Visit Elisa and her sisters to try the
different styles of Prosecco. They
serve the finest Tranquillo (still
Prosecco) here, and the Frizzante
is very refreshing, and again
something you won't find in every
winery. The tasting will be
accompanied by local cheeses.

5.30pm Maybe an opportunity to visit Osteria Senz' Oste on the
way back to your hotel, or sneak in another winery.

Osteria Senz' Oste

Outside seating with a view - Osteria Senz' Oste

Apart from my four favourite wineries listed above, I would also recommend any of the following, depending on how long you're visiting the area, where you are staying and whether you have transport.

1. Borgo Antico, Conegliano – within easy distance of Conegliano train station
2. L'Antica Quercia, Conegliano – great tasting in the vineyard
3. Vigne Matt in Cison di Valmarino – superb views from the tasting room
4. Gregoletto in Miane – lovely family atmosphere
5. Al Canevon, Valdobbiadene – good ambience
6. Colesel, Valdobbiadene – cellar environment, very welcoming
7. Vigneto Veccio, Valdobbiadene – Accommodation, food and Prosecco, within walking distance of Colesel and several other wineries
8. Adami, Vidor – superb selection of Prosecco and Rive products
9. RivaCaselle16, Vidor – Great host – Giulia is perfect at describing the products and has tons of knowledge; lovely lunch in the vineyard
10. Le Volpere, Farra di Soligo – original ideas, part of the Prosecco safari.

I hope this book has given you some ideas on where to visit on your Prosecco journey and that I've succeeded in giving you a little insight into the area. Irrespective of my explanations, if you are fortunate enough to visit you will see that I haven't really done it justice. In reality, it's so much more than I can put on paper. Everything is fabulously brilliant: the views, the area, the people and then there's the absolutely gorgeous Prosecco. As you can see, there's a lot of choice, but wherever you venture, I'm sure you will have a fantastic time. My journey continues...

Cheers!

23. ABOUT THE AUTHOR

Amanda Mohr is a Prosecco DOCG specialist and hosts Prosecco tastings and events throughout Yorkshire. These include private parties, Prosecco pairing dinners, and Prosecco sampling with afternoon tea on the Keighley & Worth Valley heritage railway.

Enthusiastic about highlighting the quality and differences of Prosecco Superiore, Amanda has visited the Prosecco DOCG region regularly over the last seven years, developing relationships with Prosecco producers and gaining a real appreciation for the area, which has led to her escorting several small groups on specialist tours.

A qualified accountant and head of finance, Amanda continues to combine her working life with her passion for spreading the word about Prosecco Superiore. She currently lives in West Yorkshire with her partner, Steve.

More information about Prosecco Superiore, parties or visiting the region can be found at www.iloveprosecco.co.uk

Printed in Great Britain
by Amazon